the space between seconds

learning to manage your own mind

n.y. haynes

atmosphere press

Published by Atmosphere Press

Cover design by Nick Courtright

Library of Congress Control Number
2020918208

The Space Between Seconds
2020, N.Y. Haynes

atmospherepress.com

CONTENTS

To our ancestors and the traditions of our heritage, for without them I'd be a mariner without an ocean.

PROLOGUE

Love is the light. Forward is the motion.
--BarbaraO

Sciences have traditionally been based on the hypothesis that the behavior of the whole can be explained in terms of properties of its components. Thereby the thought is that complexity of a system or organ could best be understood by considering the functions of its isolated parts.

The reduction behaviorist approach has had a very successful history—success with the discovery of many of the fundamental principles concerning the interactions of the parts which make up a whole. It is becoming clear, however, that there are some fundamental aspects of life which cannot be understood from this reduction behaviorist point of view.

Our body systems are never isolated, and are not free to function separately, but rather to co-ordinate their activities: to generate a unique state of dynamic order which is absent in any non-living system. Thousands of reactions are going on simultaneously to constitute the perfectly organized symphony of life—mind, body, and soul. Precise co-ordination is required at each of a number of hierarchical levels: electric, molecular, cellular, and mental—all the way across the whole system. Animal-based research omits a whole dimension of these dynamic interactions, for some of the existing questions remain unanswered if not asked. Neither did the reduction behaviorist approach explain the mechanism of ***energy*** transduction, the transduction of chemical ***energy*** into mechanical, electrical, or osmotic work.

The ***energy*** and purpose of this book is to present plainly and openly a rhythmic system of learning to manage and direct the ***energy*** of your own mind, body, and soul to the highest possible state. This can never be mastered by mere book study. One must apply this ***energy*** through rigorous surrender to self-discipline and practical training.

The Space Between Seconds is designed as an interactive journal wherein the questions are to be answered in the present, not later, but as you read them. This act of writing is educationally the best method of growth—ingesting and assimilating truth into daily living. It involves you physiologically, as well as psychologically, adding more motivation and inspirational power to your efforts.

Do not be intimidated by the supposed seriousness of keeping a meditation-training journal. Without question, recording basic facts about yourself is an immeasurable step toward *self-efficacy* and release while you read, but for the most part, this journey simply provides a space to log and free yourself from all impediments and imbalanced ***energy*** within, and encounter your mental and spiritual release without excuses.

Whatever you're looking for, there's something in here for you. No matter how seriously or casually your journey, you'll discover tremendous rewards in just jotting down your thoughts, feelings, and responses to these pages.

This approach essentially yields success in gaining increased mental, physical and spiritual power since it coordinates the mental,physical, and spiritual energies in the maintenance and development of the whole system. In many ways, how we organize and experience the flow of our ***energy*** can be different from what we previously believed about spirituality, diet, exercise, training, and ourselves.

At heart, I am an educator that loves learning and teaching equally. Knowledge is power, and strength is paramount. In that spirit, I propose this work as a humble attempt to address the serious and legitimate concern that the vast, overwhelming majority of people do not know how to get from where they are to a healthier lifestyle, and those that may have the common sense and knowledge lack the discipline.

This problem justifiably discourages many people from strength training, holistic diets, and optimal spiritual health, wherein they continue to place the health of their physiques in the reach of those foods, living patterns, and situations with a demonstrated history of abuse and abandon. In my own gratitude and commitment to results, honesty about what works, and the time-honored principles of meditation and exercise science, I trust that my efforts may be effective and satisfying in abating the health crisis.

It is my desire that your rhythmic journey through *The Space Between Seconds* will firmly, kindly, and gently guide you to a leaner, stronger physique and a greater sense of peace with spirit and joy with self. Experience shows that quality and quantity ***must*** go hand in hand. Thus I offer this hybrid personal and professional compendium of over thirty years of constant study and experience in applying these healthy principles which have been found very effective.

PART ONE:
Our Language of Thoughts and Emotions

CHAPTER ONE: INTRODUCTION TO "ENERGY" AND "THE AURA"

NEUROPLASTICITY OF THE SOUL

Thus strangely are our souls constructed,
and by such slight ligaments
are we bound to prosperity or ruin.
–Mary Shelley, *Frankenstein*

Yesterday, amid the crowd on Broadway, I felt myself jostled timorously under mysterious unknown propulsions, then abruptly, fell precipitated into a sudden wild ***energy*** where the pain and the promise of life merge with quiet in a vacuum—a quiet where impatience, restlessness and irritability intensify pain. An unmoving quiet not marked on timepieces, but rocked by the imperceptible reality, airy as a sigh. It is through mental resignation, non-resistance, and a certain stilling of the mind that I later came to surrender.

From this quiet, always the same quiet patience of spirit, my heart grows, inch by inch, as the convulsions of my soul, pressing up the emotional flames within, and the painful spasms of my young mind, my flesh, at the dusk of the Creative Source which at times feels just like holding a ghost in crowds.

Our bodies stream our souls into many areas of wonderment, wanderings, and transformations like fatigued waves breaking on the shore, radiating new horizons. It has been three days since my fiancé and I ended our relationship. Presently, I am grateful for the resources of talking to friends, prayer and meditation, and of course a willingness to help someone else.

Gratitude: pleasing; appreciative of benefits received providing pleasure or comfort; to oblige.

I am taking extra care with my immune system because of the emotional vulnerability and fatigue. It feels like I'm traipsing through thick sand as someone else, yet the process of one moment then the next, focus, gratitude, and trust are guiding me through. The major lesson is always keeping some self for the self. The fact that my ex-fiancé is cruel, immature, and a penis does not change the fact that in love I was then and am now, for I literally live in love singularly and with our romance.

The pain and the loss are tangible as I am now left with the space of positive ***energy*** that conserved the relationship. This is day two of the Apple Cleanse. The silence and the peace are deafening. I feel fabulously restored, alone and released. I noticed when I'm quiet at night, I am moaning like my soul is aching, asking, grieving, and letting go. It sounds like a cheetah (perhaps it is the sound of missing my fiancé).It is like I've been away and am returning. Yet I've been here all the while. Our natural spiritual powers are phenomenal.

Energy

The ***energy*** of forgiving totally and unconditionally opens the heart so that an unlimited abundance of love ***energy*** becomes dynamic and can flow freely. The opposite occurs when we switch off our hearts, close our minds (through resentments of past events), and pull ourselves into a darkened restrictive space within. Living in love and happiness is living in the high ***energy*** of trust and is ageless.

- Where does all your ***energy*** come from?
- Why is the ***energy*** there sometimes and at other times we are completely drained?
- Does food help when we are emotionally and mentally consumed?
- How does this happen? Where does this ***energy*** come from?

Energy is an electrical and magnetic current surrounding all that is physical. It is a measurable entity; however, it is only measurable through the examination of the potential to perform work. That is, ***energy*** is defined as the ability to perform work. So, we can say that we can only measure ***energy*** indirectly. ***Energy*** is related to the ability to produce or alter force. I apologize for the vagueness of this definition, but ***energy*** has an elusive essence:

- I know that ***energy*** is there, but it is difficult to explain where.
- I know that ***energy*** exerts an influence, but it is difficult to see exactly how.
- I know that ***energy*** is found within mass, but it is difficult to see exactly where.

Our bodies are constantly in a state of ***energy*** flux, as ***energy*** is stored and released in intervals. This ***energy*** flows into and out of our bodies, moving into and out of different tissues and molecules, being passed on in an endless succession, changing forms but never being lost. We exchange ***energy*** with the environment throughout our lives, for wherever mass is present, ***energy*** is also present.

This electrical and magnetic current surrounding all that is physical obeys the law that negative always receives and positive always transmits. In humans, male and female currents complement each other:

Male	Female
Left leg is positive	**Right leg is positive**
Right arm is positive	**Left arm is positive**
Right leg is positive	**Left leg is negative**
Left arm is negative	**Right arm is negative**

This is sometimes referred to as "your aura"—an electro bubble which extends three feet in all directions around us. This electro bubble is likened to heat waves shimmering from the earth on sizzling days. It is sensitive to colors, smells, and sounds. Furthermore, color and music are cloaks for force and play a great role in balancing the vibrating action of living cells and the glands. Our glands deposit their hormones directly into the blood stream and our bodies completely renew all cells every seven years.

Endocrine System

When your ***energy*** current is out of balance with itself, it is reflected in your endocrine hormonal system. The endocrine is one of two major communication systems within your body. One of these systems can be said to be your "wired" system; the other system can be said to be your "wireless" system.

1. Your "wired" communication system is your nervous system. It is a very

rapid system with communication occurring at great speed and the actions are dissipated without delay.

2. Your "wireless" communication system is your endocrine system. The action of hormones simply carries a message from one location to another location using a system of tubes for delivery. It takes much longer for this system to respond compared to the nervous system. The effects cannot be dissipated as rapidly and last much longer, as dissipation requires the metabolism of the hormone.

Metaphysically it's the ***energy*** radiating through our spinal cord keeping us upright. Changes in consciousness currents fall into two categories—one is a downward current, flowing from our mind to words; The other is an upward current, flowing from the ground to our mind—both of which are basic factors in self-recognition, transformation, and the healing process.

Our hormones are chemical messengers that are synthesized, stored, and released into our blood by endocrine glands. Increases in the size of skeletal muscle tissue are primarily accomplished via hormonal mechanisms. Nothing causes your body to alter its shape and size more so than hormones. Certain kinds of foods, beverages, and exercise can cause significant release of hormones. In particular, fear, resistance training, and diet can be significant stimulants of hormone production.

It is very possible that weight training may increase resistance and immunity to disease by its ***energizing*** action on the endocrine glands. Reinvigorated endocrines give our body the power to make use of vitamins and minerals, so that, by revitalizing and ***energizing*** the endocrines, weight training creates an improved state of vitamin-mineral metabolism and helps overcome nutritional deficiencies.

Additionally, there are said to be twenty-one minor concentration ***energy*** centers in our palms, soles of our feet, our knees, our fingertips and our shoulders with no noted particular gland connection. However, some research data connects them to our lymphatic system.

Lymphatic System

Our lymphatic system plays an integral role in its close relationship to our tissues regarding nourishment, assimilation, secretion, and elimination or purification. Our vasomotor arrangement in relation to the nodes and large ducts, and the nerve centers from which impulses come are a complete system within itself from our head, neck, chest, abdominal-pelvic, and inguinal regions defending against pathogens both foreign and domestic.

Balance can be defined as a healthy, functioning, self-integrated individual with life ***energies***, while expressing wellness through constant change and growth. Call your eternal ***energy*** anything you want, but you *must* call it; it is you. Your consciousness is internal ***energy.*** Think of this as a compass: one direction is for actions and the other for receiving. One seeks to understand and the other to control. Increasing our listening is receiving. When our thoughts are racing or we are mentally rehashing the past or projecting into the future, we are expending ***energy,*** which can and does lead to overeating and probably nutrition deficiency because we tend to reach for stimulants: coffee, tea, alcohol, sugar, dairy, and tobacco.

Our thoughts (recalling, creating) and emotions (disciplining, recalling) all drive our internal ***energy*** economy. This ***energy*** is neither affected nor maintained by our food sources. It is spiritually maintained and explains why sometimes you are so internally geared that food seldom crosses your thoughts. And other times you feel lethargic and heavy and eating does nothing to replenish you. The former is like being in love (open) and the latter is like being congested in fear (closed). Living from this source is living with enthusiasm. This is what is meant by living in the light.

You have the ability to turn off your internal ***energy*** and keep it ***off.*** Imagine if the only way to keep the Moon and the Sun from shining on you is to turn off the outside world. You would have to make your internal realm dark by closing all the windows, drawing the curtains, and unscrewing all the light bulbs, including the fluorescent one above the bathroom mirror. It is exactly like moonshine. The Moon and the Sun shine; that is all they do is shine. They are never late, never critical, and most importantly, never talk. All they do is shine. They shine when it's cloudy; they shine when it's storming; they are there shining. They are simply overshadowed by the ever-changing architecture of the clouds and frontal systems. Your internal ***energy*** is your enthusiasm, your love, and your joy.

- How high do you want to get?
- How much love and happiness do you want to feel?
- How much enthusiasm do you want to have for

the things you do?

CHAPTER TWO: OPENING YOURSELF TO LOVE AND HAPPINESS

EBB AND FLOW

..."My body's weak, I'm on the run no time to sleep. I've got to ride, ride like the wind to be free again.
—Chris Cross ***"Sailing"*** album

Open, open, open. If enjoying a full life means experiencing unbelievable ***energy***, love, peace, and enthusiasm all the time, then always remain open. Ask yourself:

- Who am I who can just watch emotions and thoughts come up with a complete sense of disentanglement?
- Are you willing to stay open?

Then decide to open and stay open. Period. Adhere and allow this to be your state of being.

ADHERE: from the Latin word *adhaerere,* to stick; to maintain loyalty without deviation.

ALLOW: from the Latin word *allaudare,* to praise; to give as a gift; given at regular interval for a specific purpose; to acknowledge/admit; to permit the presence of.

Train yourself to disremember and forget how to switch off!

- What triggers you?

Sounds, sights (persons, colors, things, places), smells,

tastes, and your full spectral sensorium; make a commitment to recover and discover your ability for receiving unlimited ***energy;*** for living fully in love and happiness without the pain of fear.

Deliberately eradicate layers of internal dialogue, of noise and focus on direct experiences. Let go of the onslaught of labels and conditions keeping the world at bay. These labels are used to pigeonhole all people, places, things, and experiences. This prevents the self from experiencing anything innovative, new, or surprising. We reduce the novel, the freshness of each moment to the controlled and known labels. In so doing, we divest ourselves of freshness and freedom. Our existence becomes as enthusiastic as paper left out in the rain. Relax, release, and let go of predetermined classifications and be open to experiencing first hand once again, like a toddler exploring and discovering the world.

Our minds and hearts can become locked, blocked with stored unresolved ***energy*** patterns from our past (mine was abandonment—healed now through love). Because our minds and hearts can become locked and loaded like a hamster on a wheel; its repetitive narration of resentment, anxiety, or fear about the world; only dwelling in the unknown can introduce new content. A fresh point of view can release our locked and loaded minds from their wheel of sameness.

Become a conduit. A conduit lets things happen around it. Things come to the conduit. Light. Air. Sound. It takes from everything and willingly allows everything to go. Nothing gets stuck in the conduit because everything comes into the conduit; nothing stays in the conduit; the conduit remains. How would you define a conduit? Is it everything? Is it nothing? A conduit cannot be defined; therefore, it cannot be limited. It has an identity all its own. Everything happens through a conduit.

- What is it like having everything pass right through without the meanings we attach to things, people, and places?
- What would it be like living in unconditional love and happiness as a way of life?

The Four Pillars of Love and Happiness

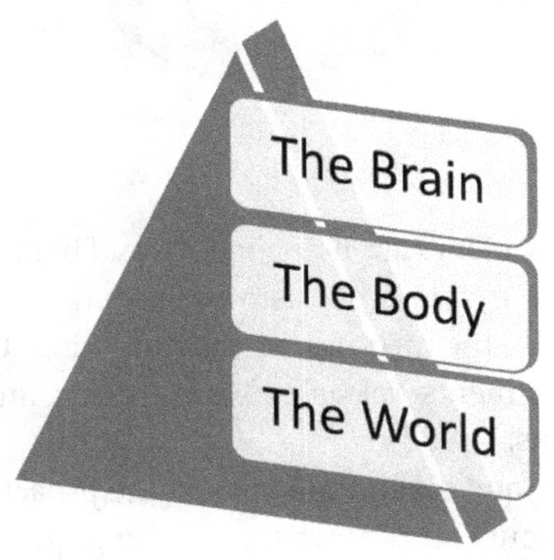

We can view our consciousness as a triangle of the brain, the body, and the world with the flow of ***energy.*** As mentioned previously, one direction seeks to control the surroundings and the other to understand. Our paying attention without attachment and letting go of everything is absolute trust, living in love and happiness without **O**bligations, **J**udgments, **E**xpectations, and **C**onditions **(OJEC).**

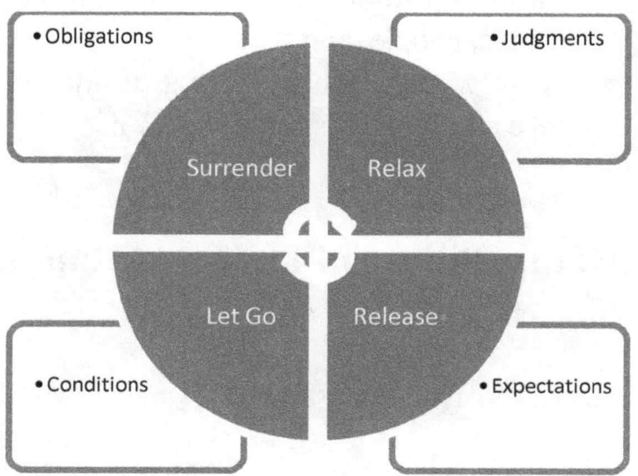

The Four Pillars are living in love and happiness not as an apex of a pyramid but as a base foundation spiraling constantly in the process of surrendering **O**bligations, relaxing **J**udgments, releasing **E**xpectations, and letting go of **C**onditions.

Training and meditation are just the proactive practice of getting out of the way, of letting go. Constantly surrender guilt, anger, fear, blame, self-pity, shame, depression, and ego; for they are all maintained through creating obligations, judgments, expectations, and conditions.

Since ***energy*** is stored as pain, guilt, blame, shame, and fear, look at how these are packaged into your life and where you carry them within. Our refusals to discover, relax, and release these takes all, or at least a large portion of, the beauty and fun out of living. We *must* learn and relearn to forgive, overcome, and have fun—by living in release and subsequent relief from the pains, the disappointments, and the misconceptions from childhood, adolescence, and adult yesterdays. This will allow a new ***energy*** pattern to vibrate and circulate within our bodies. Yes, it will be painful, but there is no growth without pain and discomfort. Plus, we only have to feel it once. When we maintain negative vibrations within us, these vibrations are repeated. This is suffering. This is struggling. Let's just do the work: feel the pain, the discomfort and go on to grow through more fun, adventure, and different ***energy*** vibrations.

Hostility prevents positive actions but when pooled with fear, indolence, avarice, self-righteousness, intolerance, and prejudice, it's used as a destructive and legitimate means of eliminating all types of life forces: plant, animal, and human. So examine your internal space.

- What are the negative states (fear, anger, prejudice, perverse victim) that arise for you most often?
- What is the psychic payoff (pleasure) that you derive from embracing your negative states or people?

Our emotions, our thoughts, and our behaviors are under our umbrella of choice, worth, and value. Begin and continue making an internal decision to regulate your life ***energy*** by training to remain like a switch in the open position instead of the off position.

Give voice to this meditation

Energy

- You *must* take time to extend yourself forgiveness and reconcile with the past.
- Forgiveness keeps our hearts soft and open. When our hearts are open and clear, our minds are open and clear enough to listen and create, unencumbered with revenge, anger, jealousy, or resentments. All of which keeps us stuck in the past or hopeless in the future.

Affirmation: Right here, right now, I am grateful for this day's ***energy.*** It is enough and I am enough. This is my sporting adventure of opened, enthusiastic joy. I am going to remain relaxed regardless of what happens. I honor my ***energy*** within. I respect it enough to let it be open always.

The pattern of forgiveness goes to and includes those patterns around how we feel, and felt, about our parents—their behaviors and attitudes—moving through to all subsequent relationships with either sex. The patterns once investigated allow for spiritual opening with a capacity to rise up, move over, and soar beyond. The full rewards of interactions are in the present as they are fabricated in love. Your love, the love that is already within, effusively propagates each action and attitude.

So embrace all of life: stay focused to your commitment and be willing to work at it, in it, through it, and around it. This is the miracle of it. By staying on this voyage, you have created unlimited abundance of opened joy, love, and excitement.

The only bad human that can steal your joy, your joy ***energy,*** is you.

Decide to investigate

- How do you want to spend the limited time you have available?
- How does the unresolved in past relationships haunt and cause reactions which block the actions of the present?

Surrender guilt, anger, fear, shame, depression, and the like; then open up, relax, create, become productive, and laugh like the Kayapȯ. The Kayapȯ, an indigenous tribe in a remote part of the Amazon rainforest, interact with the world in a captivating manner. They interpret emotional and physical injury—no matter how painful—as an absolutely comical experience, a great source of humor. They express pain through laughter. A fall or an agonizing stubbed toe—it doesn't matter. They hold dominion over their environment and how it affects them.

In a poetic reversal the Kayapȯ also translate their emotions into physical pain. A mother mourning the loss of her child (an experience I am deeply familiar with), for instance, expressed her sorrow by slicing two-inch crevices in her scalp with a machete. Upon this writing, it has been years since her son's death, but this woman's grief is still apparent. Her head is covered with long, ridged scars, which look like dried wild reeds radiating a funeral veil. That woman's sorrow resonated and reverberated my own son's death like a squeaking razor blade against my diaphragm, bending itself with each breath. Presently, when Kayapȯ fall in love, they scratch the shoulder of their partner, the object of their affection.

The deeper the love, the deeper the scratch; throughout their village, thin scars mark every man and woman who ever loved someone or ever once felt love.

How this Kayapò tribe uses their bodies to express joy and pain deeply resonated with me. It is as if they have turned their bodies inside out, displaying for the entire world to see what they are feeling internally, a heartstring to be surged. Their scratches and scarification are not cues to some mysterious inner ailment; they are the feelings themselves, made manifest, visible, and as such, readily identifiable, not unlike tears from our eyes.

Thus interpreting how the Kayapò manage physical sensations and emotions simultaneously, as if they are one and the same, helped to heighten my personal experience of the world because the Kayapò understand there is always pain: pain of ailments, death, growing and grief, all of which are part of the promise of life. But it is our response to such promises that matters most.

The very real *energy* of the stored past creeps up or lives intermittently in current relationships: something or someone stimulates it (it can be a voice, a smell, a movie, a song), then suddenly you become moody, irritated, and restless. Your heart rate has increased from unfinished and unresolved patterns. It is like living in a loop which occupies too large a percentage of your present. Once this process is consummated, you can live in your relationships fully and totally nonresistant like water.

And just like water releases, purifies and cleanses, this will be the new pattern of loving; in this manner, easing the challenge of being open to, and beginning new relationships. This is a lifetime practice. You will embrace the beauty and the glory of an unpolluted horizon—new sparkling diamonds of ***energy*** within. I use diamonds, as they are the hardest substance. Only another diamond can scratch a diamond, and even amid scratches, they are beautiful, like the Kayapó.

When we feel uninspired in life, as though nothing is going right, it is often because we are holding something back. We all have a tendency to hedge our bets, to put forth a full effort. Even when we do exert ourselves in some area of life, we tend to set limits ahead of time; at once creatively and physiologically initiating stress and tension of our ***energy*** subconsciously. Our subconscious is fertile soil, it does not discriminate. Spiritual growth, and subsequently on-going maturity, is about changing and living through, and in, the love ***energy*** within. And change is constant as well as dark sometimes!

The purpose of our spiritual growth and maturity is to delete the blockages which cause us fear. Life assists us by placing situations and people to inspire our growth. Once that is done, if it is a relationship, they move on, they leave our lives. Romantic ones hurt more only when we try to hold on past their expiration date. It's like a child in the womb when the water breaks (tears), birth is imminent.

Fear is the antithesis of change. One who lives with a lot of fear despises change and therefore strives to create an environment about them that is definable, controllable, and predictable, forgetting that predictability is boring and has side effects of its own. This exacerbates our body's deterioration not only from its inherent material transitory nature, but additionally, when we do not care for it properly through nutritionally dense diet and exercise—and when we do not pause and make amends for harms committed against others and ourselves. To live beyond surface spirituality we surrender, surrender, and re-surrender to being open, letting go and growing to gently work with our places of resistance, making small changes whenever possible.

Amazing things only begin to happen when we give beyond reason and cease holding back. When it motivates and feels good, do it and do it some more—do our best always. Trust the process, and our best comes through naturally. Then we just leave it alone with no thought of the results (working, running, cycling, love-making, ET cetera.). The rewards of patient rhythmic training slowly build and maintain confidence while nurturing serenity, stillness, optimism and trust. When you own a body that trusts you, these become the key ingredients of love, happiness, and power.

When we surrender, surrender, surrender, remarkable things begin to happen. We shift from over-active consumers (over-buying, -eating, -sitting, -sexing, -texting, etc.) to unlimited access to our productive creative ***energy*** fully fueled by love and happiness. Our creative ***energies*** respond to our self-confidence (faith) in their capacity and resilience. Fear drastically undermines this capacity (programming for self-destruction).

Remember the bondage of self (ego, delusion), self-concept (psychological survival instinct, flight or fight...run...run...run), outside struggles with your own internal fears, insecurities, self-destructive (programmed-patterned ***energy***) attitude and behavior patterns all are flows of channeling ***energy***.

Only you can, and are responsible for your freedom

and your love. External reactions to the internal rise of heart rate (flight or fight run, run, run or hell, hell, hell) cause a discombobulating freeze. Physiologically there is no running, thus an internal shut-down, withdrawal, and retreat behind your armor. You disappear behind a defensive shield. It has the effect of alcohol on the alcoholic that is hypersensitive and too receptive to the internal environmental signals of various sensorial ***energies*** entering and causing fear. Pulling a shell around them (like a tortoise), the parts that are most vulnerable, that are weak. We are only as strong as our weakest link.

Recall that fear shunts our ***energy*** patterns from higher vibrancies and thought patterns to primal/survival threatened mode. You have a choice. You can pause and allow that fear-based ***energy*** to simply walk on by. You are the only balm and salve for your freedom from fear and imposed limitations and your freedom to be all that you already are within.

Do you feel like someone is out to get you? Great, let them have you. What will they do with you? Let it go, let them have your goat. If you don't want your fear, don't defend it. Then you are open and living in love mentally, creatively, and physically. You can be joyful, spontaneous, enthused, and excited. Waltzing through open, relaxed to keep your ***energy*** moving. It is the spontaneous service of living in love and happiness without expecting anything in return: the service itself is the reward.

Thoughts and emotions are just objects of consciousness. When your heart rate is altered, you are aware. Who is aware? It is the Self. Whenever you sense changes in your ***energy*** pattern, condition yourself to pause and relax behind this. Pause, breathe deeply, and feel the physiological ***energy*** which ***energizes*** and electrifies from each breath. Living in love and happiness: **OJEC** – no controlling, criticizing, fighting, struggling, fixing, or changing. "Just let it be." Surrender, relax, release and let it go! Then observe. It works, it really does.

The body and the mind function best when they have been given a chance to begin again. When we train and meditate, we are seeking to return the body and the mind to clarity so that it will be ready for the next activity. We have a pretty good idea of the activities in life that make us happy, sane, and well adjusted.

The objects of consciousness come and go like dark and bright, for at the center of light is darkness and at the center of darkness is light. The consciousness watches as emotions and thoughts come and go. It is our constant and simply sees all and knows all about you. This consciousness has the clarity to see from whence they came and to whence they go without thinking about them.

See your thoughts rising like a front of clouds coming over the horizon. In order to reset your mind, do not inquire into the thoughts. Pay more attention to the empty spaces between the thought clouds instead of the thoughts. If the devil is in the details, then so is the divine!

Relationships don't work very well (especially with yourself) when you are not centered. You are all over the place: the next one, the next thing, the next thought.

When scattered, it usually is very difficult to maintain a healthy and productive life, for when we are scattered, nutrition, exercise and prayer, and meditation are arduous because the internal channels of ***energy*** are stressed.

The shifting ***energy*** drowns us, and like an eddy, we

are drawn hopelessly into its spinning force. Thus consciousness is adrift internally and externally while we are wide awake, making us asleep. Our consciousness is adrift because our power has been averted and siphoned away through our focus—or more so—lack of focus. Focus is a feeding power—***energy***. Thus, when we feel ourselves becoming defensive, our offense is to release. Relax and let it waltz on by like clouds moving over the horizon.

Even while experiencing great losses, deep inside you are centered and consciously let go, release, and move through. For example: We (Inner Teacher) had a positive mammogram which required a subsequent biopsy. We gracefully moved into a state of deep meditation. Through this state We remember the doctor saying, "You are so calm, most people are anxious and worried." We listened and said nothing, remaining in a spine-centered color meditation.

Life is life

Fear is resistance to change and growth.

- Is your image of the divine serving you or causing harm?
- Why do you need the events of life to be a particular way?
- How did you develop the notion that life is not all right just the way it is, or that it will not be all right the way it shall be?
- Who said that the way life naturally unfurls is not all right?

Fear, that part of you that is not all right with itself, says so. If you are outlining divinity and creation based upon the most unpleasant part of your being, what do you expect them to look like? They are going to look like a dreadful chaos. Is your image of the divine serving you or causing you harm? Pause for a few minutes and think about what it might feel like to be completely surrounded with love and devotion.

As you grow spiritually, you see that your attempts to defend yourself from your problems actually manifest problems. The healthy alternative is to *decide* to cease fighting anything and everything. Simply cease fighting with life for this is an act of insanity. Accept that life is not under your control. Life is constantly changing, and if you are trying to control it, you will never be able to *fully* live it.

There exists such a thing as a life without fear. First you must understand fear itself. When you have fear inside you, the events of life invariably stimulate it. *Life creates situations that push you to your edges,* all with the effect of removing what is congested inside of you. Whatever is congested and suppressed within you forms the roof of fear. *Fear is caused by congestions in the flow of* ***energy,*** and when your ***energy*** is congested, it's incapable of rising up to nourish your heart. Thus, your heart becomes undernourished. When your heart is undernourished, it becomes susceptible to lower vibrations, like a thrombosis in a plaque filled artery, and of the lowest vibrations is fear.

Fear appears to be such a painful, frightening experience that people do practically everything to avoid and control it. People will do almost anything to avoid pain and to resist pain because pain ignites fear, and fear enervates and triggers the flame at the wick of hatred, anger, and a desperation handled adroitly by withdrawing into society and further pandering to your fears.

The media plays inside your fears (be aware). Loss of fear is always a growth opportunity. Know your wants. Know your needs. You are hard-wired to avoid and to resist pain, not so much to seek pleasure, but to avoid pain and run, run, run. Be wise and thoughtful about your pain. Ask yourself before you run:

- Is this good for my long term growth?
- At the point of pain, do you flee and plea, "let me go," or do you surrender and move with its flow?

Fear is the cause of every problem. It is the root of all prejudices and the negative emotions of anger, jealousy, and possessiveness of people, places, and things. If you had no fear, if you lived in love, you could be perfectly happy living in this world. Nothing would unsettle you. You would be willing to face everything and everyone simply because you wouldn't have fear inside of you that could cause you disturbance.

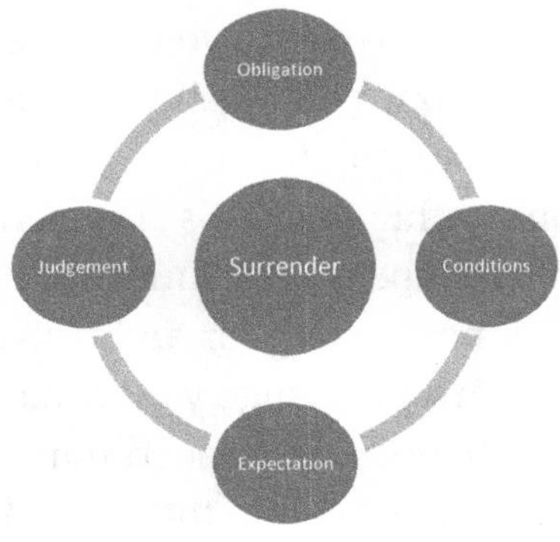

The Four Pillars of Love and Happiness lived in combination with the principles of Rhythmic Training (presented in Part Two) enables you to fearlessly dance in the constant circle of change spiraling in the process of *surrendering **O**bligations, relaxing **J**udgments, releasing **E**xpectations, and letting go of **C**onditions*. When and if you desire, you can sing, "I can see clearly now the FEAR is gone. I can see all obstacles in my way." All of the dark ***energies*** that had me congested... "It's 'gonna be a bright, bright" fulfilling life!

- When was the last time you felt so happy that you danced for joy?
- What can help recapture that feeling in your heart of celebration and joy?

When we live in love—true love—we have no obligations, for we trust that love is what it is.

A session with a Seeker once began:

EXCERPT

"How have you been?"

"Busy. Having some work done in my house. The contractor keeps saying, 'You'll change your mind.' Why do they always come zooming around when I just get my life the way I want it. What do you call that?"

"I don't know, but relationships are a lot of work, so let's call it 'machismo' for our session. Maleness or manliness won't define this. This is something else."

"This always happens each time that I say I'm content with myself, I'm not looking for an involved relationship. He keeps saying, 'You'll change your mind.'

"Briefly, my fiancé and I ended our relationship and currently I'm endeavoring into the beyond of it. But when he and I first met—I see it clearly as we speak—I told him, ‘I have many facets of my wholeness, so many colors.’

“He said, ‘Oh, that’s okay, I understand.’ But inevitably, it came a time when I wanted and needed to be apart to write, and there was a problem. And the other clear incident was at the pond. I asked him did he want me to be a guide in his life or have an intimate relationship because I couldn’t be both, and relationships are a lot of work. He said, ‘No, no, a relationship because relationships are not work. They are fun.’ And at the point of challenge in our relationship he said, ‘You were right, relationships are a lot of work!’ And he bailed. He chose to leave, to run rather than get deeper and work through. It is all a choice.”

Our session then focused on relationships—all relationships.

“It’s always when I’m feeling powerful that this happens. They are coming at me from all directions,”

We laughed.

“That’s the way it works. They are attracted to your light—your power. All bugs are attracted to the light. They don’t know they’re just being bugs.”

“Like your relationship you were sharing about?”

“Yes. There was no other human capable of connecting the way we connected at that time. It has brought me to the depth and texture of here, now, this meditation session with you. Just look at it as the spark of life: ‘machoism,’ because he is just swimming, swimming against the other sperms. He hears your voice and your words, but he’s swimming and swimming towards what he sees, what he wants—you. And in no way is he listening. He’s hearing because just the vibration of your voice motivates his swimming, not his listening."

We laughed, "This is machoism!" We shared little chuckles.

"When the sperms swim to the egg they're all ramming their head against the egg but only one will get through, just one."

Excited she said, "Oh, that's a good analogy, and I get to pick which one. It's like I'm a red light. Why are they doing this? You said it—attraction to the light."

We laughed. We began this with the Four Pillars of Love and Happiness. They are living without Obligations, Judgments, Expectations, Conditions, **OJEC** for short.

The Seeker asked, "Well, are you saying that in a union, romantic relationship that the other person is not obligated to you and can run around with others?"

"No. I'm saying that being in love within yourself, you trust that the other person is in love within and will do what's best. His fooling or running around is not a thought to contend with."

"I can see judgment and how that is unhealthy in any relationship, especially family, but all relationships. I can't see how this is true in a union with your mate."

"Well, 'in love' as a responsibility is beyond that."

"So, you're saying responsibility gives them the right to not be obligated?"

"No. I'm saying that it is your responsibility to attend to your rights: spiritually and emotionally within. Okay let's use an outside example: people. Someone says you have the right to be free and the right to be prosperous and have the best of things. But that makes you responsible to exercise and work with your gifts, talents, and abilities to deliver those rights; it is not up to someone else. They are not responsible—we are."

She paused, agitatedly, "Okay, so I can kind of see that you're saying my relationship is a reflection of myself."

"With absolute certainty, your mate is your mirror."

"So, I don't have the right to expect that they are true or love me?"

"No. Living in love has no expectations. Each encounter is a separate entity. It only lives now in moments past."

"So, you're saying in love means the person is not obligated and I should have no expectations."

"Ahh, that word."

"What word, 'should'?"

"Absolutely, that word is full of venom. I don't 'should' on anyone and I don't allow anyone to 'should' on me."

"Okay I would..."

"Ahh, ahh."

"Well, how do you say it?"

"Pause. Breathe in through your nose, out through your mouth, and then pose your question."

Moments passed. She was breathing and silent and finally asked, "How do you say it?"

"That's just it, I live it. They are not responsible, or obligated, or expected to be and do anything but receive the love I am offering and vice versa. I just trust that they are in love within, and I am open. I am in love, living it. It is a foundation, the pillar **OJEC** sustaining itself. It is self-sustaining, radiating outward and so is your mate's."

"What about condition?"

"That's it. To expect is to put a condition on, because I love you, you must do xyz. No. I have no words to express it to you beyond this. As I said before, relationships are work!"

Unwillingly resigned, the seeker said, "Okay, this is deep, very deep. I'll try to wrap my head around it. But with family they love me, they should, I mean don't I have the right to expect?"

"No, absolutely not and I'll share an emotional betrayal example with you in a moment. But no, because I'm the one that made a decision to delve deeper into this voyage of greatness within that required blazing a new channel, different from my family. Yes. I wanted them to support me, even see and understand, but they have a choice just like I have a choice. So I am on this voyage, and they are not. The trail is there; I'm blazing it. They can choose to come, but they are not expected or obligated. They do judge and have harshly judged and criticized all my life, yet here we are having this session."

"So you mean it's me, it's not them?"

"You said it. With familial relationships expectations can easily become premeditated resentments."

"Oh, I thought, I think they are the ones and it's me. This is deep, very deep."

"This makes you responsible. Pain...go towards the pain, the discomfort if you will. We are conditioned to run from pain, run to pleasure. You know, I'm a sprinter and I'm not—nor will I ever be—that fast."

"I don't run from things, I work them through."

"I'm saying as a society, we are conditioned to head in the other direction; if something is painful within, we hide inside or some outside. Pain is not painful. Hiding in or from it, or shaming, or blaming it is painfully running to pleasure. Not so much for the pleasure in itself but to get away from the pain. The ones we've talked about before."

I then shared a recollection about emotional betrayal and forgiveness:

"The day my son died, my sisters laughed at me. This was background to the pain, anguish and sorrow nibbling at my heart, body and mind. In the foreground, years passed, as they do, and an occasion presented itself that I made amends to my sisters for behaviors of direct and indirect harms committed during our growing-up together years.

"In this fashion, I'd never really thought about the event on my son's passing, until I grew to a point in my spiritual life where I was stagnated. Then upon close examination on my anger towards death and love of my son, I discovered a strange twist around the events of that day. A death of a different kind: my trust in closeness to humans, but especially women."

The Seeker commented about my sisters, "They were jealous of you and relished in your pain! Wow! I never really understood jealousy, still do not. Because anything anyone else has I can have, as abundance is available to all for the taking."

"Fine, this is what happened, but I was still trapped spiritually, for I was anchored to my sisters through that event. To release them, I began a process of deep emotional cleansing to:

a) uncover where I was at fault;
b) open myself to a painstaking voyage of repair, reconciliation and realignment of any and all the destruction; and
c) learn how to reconstruct the best relationship for all concerned: aligning, redefining and preparing through transition.

"I had my implements of disability that culminated in a basic inability to release them and thereby unchain my spiritual stagnation to grow once more. I prayed for help in making, preparing, and transitioning. For many days, I read my prayer, concentrated on my sisters, and then one afternoon I was moved to a space of opened rawness and a feeling of walking through a boggy mud within, yet outwardly walking at a reasonably fast pace.

"Upon returning home, I reclined in the middle of my bed, curled up in a fetal position and cried: tears of release, cleansing and purposeful desire. I don't know how long I remained there, but when I arose, I felt light, poised and...truly there are no words to describe it. It would be lost in translation. Today, I call them sister A and sister B, and I am totally at peace with this.

"Who would have thought that being open and willing to accept(acknowledge with responsibility) and reconcile the pain of sister A and sister B's emotional betrayal, by forgiving(letting go and restoring) the hurt in my being could lead directly to the violent untwisting of a stored emotional pattern dishonoring and conflicting my consciousness?

"Progressing through this process of violent untwisting and detangling laid out exactly how I had, and was emotionally betraying myself. And now I had to choose, post the reconciliation and receiving of healing, I could either embrace, respect and venerate this more intense access to my love—the ***energy*** that I am, or go on to the bitter-end of my human existence slumped, hovering in a position of poison that seduces and deceives from within. I chose to rise more, shine more, and radiate more openly in the power of *love*. This is my 'hole'—living holiness. Like a hole everything passes through because I am open—a conduit—available because of self-understanding, celebration, and nurturing. That emotional blockage was my weakest link siphoning away the power from everything I touched. Sometimes quickly, sometimes slowly, but always siphoning.

"Succinctly, I share with you that somewhere at the commencing of my voyage, I made a decision, not a resolve, for resolutions like at New Year's require no actions, just verbiage. A decision to delete temporarily—no time limits, just trusting that they'd be returned and they have—these words from my vocabulary: hard and easy (because they usually come as a pair), right and wrong (another pair), and good and bad (because this pair has been immanent since childhood).

"The greatest take away about forgiveness was and is that when someone understands there is no explanation necessary and when they don't there is none possible.

"I no longer have the time or the ***energy*** to hide. As a matter of fact, post the event about sister A and sister B and forgiveness, there've been greater levels of innovation and soaring in fear-free living. I'd asked...Why am I hiding? What am I hiding? Why am I ashamed? I no longer am. Afraid I am no longer. I know there is a life possible without fear, as I am living it. It's what we've been talking about—fear-free. Fear is learnt and taught. I had no idea this is what was through and beyond that deep twisted emotional betrayal portal, but here I live stronger with access to an abundance of power and profuse ***energy***. Like that song, 'I can see clearly now' the fear 'is gone. I can see all obstacles in my way.' Gone are the dark cloud ***energies*** that had me congested... 'It's gonna be a bright' ...er, more fulfilling life!"

The Seeker then smiled and queried, "How do you? How am I supposed to do this?"

"The way you did. Pause. Breathe and watch. Now you will be aware as a resultant of our session, for a seed has been planted, and it is there. Because you have initiated it, it will come to the foreground."

"I know there are laws, but this one..." she said with prayerful vulnerability.

"I'm so glad we had this meditation. Who said meditation is quiet? There are all kinds."

"Thank you."

"My pleasure! You'll be attracted to the machismo sperm guy that distracts you the most. This is not a willful act. It is a call to greater growth. All relationships are. Like my broken engagement I described to you: my try, overcome and beyond love man, he will have found the back door to your comfortable, content, alone time, and *voila*: The sperm and the egg unite—a gamete has begun and the rest you know—shared growth."

We laughed and ended our session.

Living in the Solution

For many consciousness practitioners, relaxing, releasing, and letting go seems as wrapped in mystery as alchemy, but in clear no-nonsense language: our minds are like eyes. Although the eye itself is happier when shut, it has to open to be of any use. When I've asked other seekers how it felt to have moved into a place of living ***OJEC*** in their lives: "marvelous," "phenomenal," "delectable." They often say, "The world is so vivacious again."

So use this voyage. Through your interactions with these pages a seed is being planted. You are initiating a deeper awareness, and because of this, opportunities will come to the foreground at some time when you'll find it inconvenient. Those instances will become openings for your incorporation. It will challenge you and fill you with compassion for both yourself and for others.

We have mined, worked through the pain, trudged through the purification of tears and came up with a lode. Our encounters afford a chance to give it away in its entirety. Spiritually placing us fully opened and vulnerable to love and move in the beyond. We live in surrender. We are surrendering all of this to you. So we can re-surrender to the unknown. This is the law: surrender to relaxing, releasing, and letting go. Always surrendering, beginning again, and cyclically beginning. Begin with your seed. Surrender to it and see where it takes you. Enjoy the process!

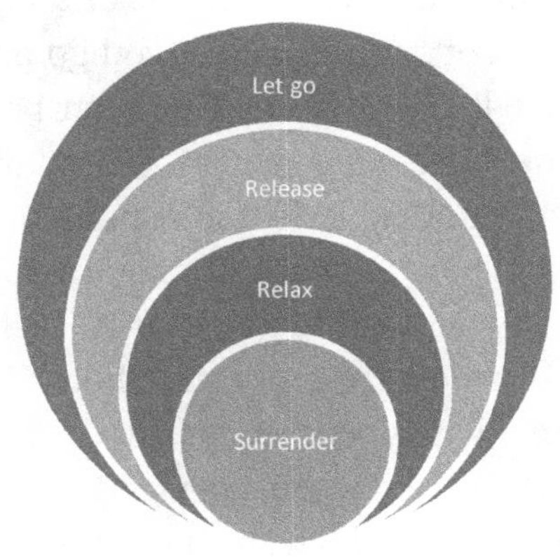

Spiritually, the law is the exact amount of time you hold on to something (thought, emotion). The exact amount of time it takes to relax, release and surrender. You'll learn this in your process, and once learnt, you'll allow its truth to govern you (this cannot be taught). When you meet this truth, you'll surrender immediately. Because you want to live in the newness of your awakenings:

- Be aware that there is something within you requiring clearance.
- You must be aware that only you, the you who notices, is separate from what you're experiencing (I call this being blinded by your own light), and
- The you that is aware is your in-love center and only from here can you surrender.

Now from the time you learn and learn to live in surrender, your new seed will be a magnet. At some point, you'll return to your surrender space and be able to see you were pulled away and into whatever emotion, drama, or object—adrift. How long you stay adrift is totally up to you: a year, an hour, three months, or a lifetime.

When you return, where did you go and how did you return? But when this seed dies from being a seed and becomes a new growth you can become the watcher and actively choose not to get lost instantaneously.

- How low on the vibrancy frequency of ***energy*** do you want to go? Fear is the lowest.
- How long will you stay there—a lifetime?

Just immediately surrender, and your ***energy*** will maintain and ascend the vibrancy and will not weaken and descend. Always look forward, never back. Regardless of what vibratility happens below you, do not lose your focus. Release, relax.

CHAPTER THREE: PAIN, STRAIN, AND FEAR

ENERGY OF RESISTANCE

> Men ought to know that from nothing else but the brain come joys, delights, laughter and sports, and sorrows, griefs, despondency, and lamentation. All these things we endure from the brain.
> —Hippocrates, *On the Sacred Disease*

It is astounding to observe what we end up doing with our will. We actively assert our will in opposition to the ***energy*** of life. If something happens that we disapprove of, we resist it. But since what we're resisting has already occurred, what benefit is it to resist? If your boyfriend or parent betrays you, it is reasonable that you disapprove. But your internal resistance to this betrayal for years to come does not change the fact that they did, indeed, betray you. It does not do anything to the reality of the situation.

Actually, it cannot even be argued that we're resistant to the actual situation. For instance, if somebody says something that we dislike, obviously our resistance won't stop them from having said it. What we're actually resisting is the experience of the event moving through us. We don't want it affecting us internally. We know it is going to create emotional and mental reactions that will not gel with what's already in there. So we assert the power of will against the effect of the event in an attempt to control it and stop it from moving through our body, and our mind. In other words, the experience of an event does not end with our sensory observation of it. The event also has to move through the soul at an ***energetic*** level. This is a process we experience daily. The initial sensory observation touches our emotional and mental ***energy*** frequencies, creating fluctuation in the ***energy.*** The fluctuations move through the soul much like the physical impact of waves through water.

Astoundingly, you truly have the power to resist these fluctuations of ***energy.*** The assertion of willpower can end the ***energy*** transfer, and that's what creates stress and tension. You can make yourself weary and fatigued resisting the experience of a single event, or even a single emotion or thought. And you know that all too well, don't you?

In the end you'll see that the resistance is a huge waste of ***energy.*** The reality is you're mostly using your will to resist one of two things: that which has already happened, or that which hasn't happened yet. You are seated inside resisting effects from the past or thoughts about the future. Think about how much ***energy*** is squandered consistently talking about or resisting what has already happened. Because the event has already passed, you are actually resisting yourself, not the event. Furthermore, ***energy*** is squandered resisting what might happen. Since most of the things you think might happen rarely or never do, you are simply rejecting your ***energy.***

How you handle your ***energy*** stream has a major effect on your life. If you assert your will against the ***energy*** of an event that has already happened (the news, social media, newspapers), it is like trying to stop the waves caused by a pebble dropped into a still lake.

Anything you do causes more interruption, not less. When you resist, the ***energy*** is blocked. It gets stuck in your soul and critically affects you. It switches off your heart's ***energy*** current and causes you to feel congested and less vibrant. This is literally what is happening when something is weighing on your spirit and mind or when things simply get too dark and gloomy for you.

This is the human plight. Events have happened and we continue to hold their ***energy*** internally by resisting or resuscitating them. Now, when we encounter today's challenges, we are neither prepared to ingest them nor capable of assimilating them. This is because we are wedged in the past ***energies.*** Strenuously, the ***energies*** can build up to a point that a person becomes so congested, they either explode or implode. This is what it means to get stressed out or even have a breakdown.

There is no reason to get distressed. There is no reason for exploding or imploding. If you do not let this ***energy*** become congested inside you, but instead, allow each moment of each day to glide through you, then you can be as ***energetic*** every moment as you might be on a stress-free trip. It is not life's events that are causing troubles or distress. It is your resistance to life's events that is causing this distress. Since the trouble is caused by using your will to resist the reality of life gliding through you, the solution is obvious—relax, release and let go. You are not in control. If you are going to resist something, at least have some sound basis for resisting. Otherwise, you are senselessly squandering valuable ***energy.***

Become willing to examine your process of resistance. In order to resist, you first *must* decide that someone or something is not the way you like it. Plenty of events and people pass right through you. Why did you decide to resist this one? Something internally *must* have a basis for deciding when to simply let things move through and when to assert willpower to either shove them away or adhere to them. There are a million things that don't bother you at all. You travel to work daily, and you hardly notice the buildings and trees. The metal on elevators doesn't stress you out at all. You see them, but they move right through you. Don't assume, however, it's that way for everyone. It's apparent that not all of us resist the same things or have the same issues. This is because we don't all have the same preconceived ideas, prejudices, and proclivities as to how things are supposed to be or how much they are supposed to matter to us.

If you want to understand stress, begin by understanding that you carry around with you your own set of preconceived ideas, prejudices, and proclivities of how things are supposed to be. It is based upon these ideas, prejudices, and proclivities of how things are supposed to be that you assert your will to resist what has already happened.

- Where did you get these preconceived ideas, prejudices, and proclivities?

Let's say that seeing bees buzzing around flowers causes you distress. Certainly that doesn't bother most people. Why does it bother you? All we need to know is that you once had a lover who harvested bees, and she broke up with you during the summer. Now every time you see bees buzzing around flowers, your heart switches off. You don't even want to go near the things; they simply create too much congestion for you.

These personal events that occur in our lives leave reactions in our minds and souls. These reactions become the basis for asserting our will to either resist or adhere. It's no more profound than that. The events may have happened in your childhood or at various points throughout your life. Regardless of why they happened, they left a reaction internally. In the immediate present, based on these past reactions, you are resisting the current events that are happening. This creates internal distress, turbulence, chaos, resistance, and anguish. Instead of accepting this and refusing to allow these past events to dominate your life, you give them power. Supposing they have real meaning, you place all your heart and soul into either resisting or adhering. But in reality, this whole process has no true meaning. It simply destroys your full enjoyment of living in love and happiness.

The alternative is to use life to relax, release, and let go of these reactions and the distress they create. In order to do this you *must* become aware, open, and willing. You *must* carefully observe this mental voice that tells you to resist something. It literally controls you: "How dare she say that. I'll show her." It gives you advice and tells you to confront the world by resisting or revisiting things.

- Why do you listen to it?
- What will happen if you cease listening?

Let your spiritual voyage become the willingness to let whatever happens move through you, rather than carrying it into the next moment. This doesn't mean you don't process what happens. You're welcome to process it, *BUT FIRST RELAX AND LET THE **ENERGY** MOVE THROUGH YOU.* If you don't, you will not actually be processing the current event, you will be processing your own congested ***energies*** from the past. You will not be responding from a space of clarity, but from a space of internal resistance, distress, and reaction. This resistance creates distress which creates knots of tension that strangle the heart physiologically and the soul spiritually.

To keep away from this, start processing each situation with acceptance. Acceptance means that events can move through you without reaction or resistance. When an event occurs and is able to move through your soul, you will be left one-on-one with the actual situation as it exists. Because you are processing the actual event, rather than stored ***energies*** kindled by the event, you won't assert reactive ***energy*** from your past.

Processing is a response in the present; reaction is in the past. You will discover that you are able to process daily situations better. It is actually possible to never have another trouble for the rest of your life. This is because events are no troubles; they're just events. Your reaction and resistance to them is what causes trouble. But, again, don't think that since you accept reality it means you don't process things. You do process them. You simply process them as events that are happening on gravitational spaceship Earth, and not as personal troubles.

You will be amazed to find that in most situations there's nothing to process except for your own desires and fears. Desire and fear make anything look complicated. If you don't have desire or fear about an event, there's nothing to process. You simply allow life to evolve and work together with it in an organic and balanced fashion. When the next thing happens, you are completely present in that moment and fully enjoying life. There are no troubles. It's all about no troubles, no distress, no strain, and no breakdown. When the events of gravitational spaceship Earth move through you, you have arrived at a deep spiritual space. You can then be totally conscious in the presence and understanding of whatever happens, without creating ***energy*** congestion. When you arrive at this space, everything becomes crystal clear. In contrast, everybody else is attempting to process the world around them while stressing with their own resistance and reactions and personal preference.

- What are your deepest fears and personal resistance?
- Today are you willing to surrender your desire to be in control, which causes your fear?
- When a person is processing their own fears, anxieties, and desires, how much ***energy*** is left for processing what's really happening?
- If this is happening in a relationship, how much time, attention, and closeness is actually being offered up?

Our desires must be inclusive so that they have freedom to vacillate with precision between the energies of the divine and the tangible. Without this, desire selects its object, whether physical or intellectual, and pursues it with rigidity.

These energies exemplify the spiritual innocence of childhood–ensconced in the familiar, but penetratingly aware of the unknown. Thus like the innocent playfulness of lovers, desire's ***energies*** can be surprisingly fertile and creatively produce delight to deepen our enjoyment of living.

Pause and give thought to what you're capable of accomplishing. Up to this point, your capacities have been inhibited by constant internal entanglements. Envision what may happen when your consciousness and understanding is liberated and free to concentrate only on the event happening now. You may have internal stillness. When you live like this, you can do anything. Your capabilities may be exponential compared to what you've ever experienced. When you can bring this level of consciousness and clarity to everything you do, your life may be altered.

So, as part of your voyage, take on this work of using life to relax, release and let go of your resistance. Relationships are a wonderful way to work with the self. Imagine if you used relationships to get to know other people, rather than to gratify what is congested inside of you. When you're not insisting that people fit into your preconceived ideas, prejudices and proclivities of what you like and dislike, **OJEC**, you will discover that relationships are not actually that complicated. When you're not actively reacting, resisting, and judging people based upon what is congested inside of you, you will discover that they are much simpler to get along with—and so are you. Relaxing, releasing, and letting go of yourself is the simplest way to get closer to people.

The same is true in your daily work. Daily work is an adventure. Truthfully, it's simple. Your work is just what you do with yourself during the day while you're here on gravitational spaceship Earth. If you desire to be content and have the full enjoyment of your work, you *must* relax, release, and let go of yourself and allow events to stream through you. Your real work is what is left to do after all else moves through.

Once the personal ***energies*** move through you, the

world becomes a new place. People and events will seem changed to you. You will understand that you have gifts, talents, and abilities you never knew before. Your entire outlook on life will change. Every single thing in the world will appear transformed. This happens because as you relax, release, and let go in any situation, it affects your clarity for other situations. For instance, let's say you have a fear of dogs. You begin to understand that other people do not have this fear, and they make it through life. Since you've had this fear for most of your life, you were full of angst while others weren't. That angst has no benefit. So you make a decision to work with your fear and relax, release, and let go when you see a dog. The way to work with resistance is by relaxing and releasing.

FACING, TRACING, AND ERASING Example A

I chose this example because I personally disliked and had a fear of dogs. I traced it back to childhood: I had a puppy, Nippy, that I absolutely adored, and one day, he just disappeared (we learnt later he was stolen). I was broken beyond belief. One day I was listening to my ex-fiancé, and once again heard his tremendous love for dogs, and this activated me to take this aversion to another level.

I prayed about this aversion and released it. Then my masseur, Kato, relocated, and I had to go through the process of finding another. While on the phone with the spa manager, she mentioned a new masseur: "There is GS; he's blind so he has his dog in the sessions with him, but he sits in the corner."

He was the only one available on the specific day I

required. My first thought was I'll have to book some other time. And the response that came out of my mouth was, "I'll book with GS."

In trying out this new masseur, who had a Labrador retriever as his companion, I am totally more present. During the session when the tension of my trapezius muscles and the knots from writing were working themselves through by deep-tissue manipulation (my favorite), my breaths became verbal. It's a pain-like sound, but it's actually my body's language from deep within letting go!

Let's back track, I was moved to give GS a hug as an introduction. Why, I have no idea.

He commented, "You have such a joyous spirit."

Subsequently, during the deep verbal release his dog was licking my left hand then rubbing his head against my hand.

Amazing! First, as mentioned, I do not particularly care for dogs, but I was thinking prior to that moment about Nippy, my puppy that was stolen. Second, because I listened when my ex-fiancé and I were conversing about his love for dogs and ownership of several in his lifetime when he said, "It's your loss." That and my other events led up to this day's event.

I kept thinking intermittently. Life...Life, gratitude for the bringing of change! I purposely chose this appointment date of the 24th because it is my deceased maternal grandmother's birthdate. And I accept all the spiritual help available without resistance. Additionally, this is the last day of the Apple Cleanse (presented in the chapter on Cleansing).

After the massage GS asked, "How do you feel?"

"Restored!"

He laughed and said, "It's amazing because you are."

The very act of relaxing and releasing through my personal resistance not only altered my relationship with dogs; it altered my relationship with everything. My soul has now learned and relearned to let congesting ***energy*** move through.

So, the next time somebody says or does something you dislike, you can unconsciously treat it the same as you would the fear of dogs. This process of relaxing and releasing through resistance adds an advantage to everything in your life. This is because it directly focuses on how to keep your heart open and willing when it is trying to switch off.

Deep internal release is a spiritual voyage in and of itself. It is the voyage of nonresistance, the voyage of acceptance, the voyage of surrender. It's about not revisiting or resisting ***energies*** as they move through you. If you find this challenging, do not beat up on yourself. Just continue working with it. It's the work of a lifetime to become that open, that whole, and that complete.

A solution is to simply practice relaxing and releasing, and handle only what's in front of you. You don't need to stress about the rest. When you relax and release, you will observe how it puts you through awesome spiritual growth. You'll begin to feel an immeasurable ***energy*** develop internally. You will feel much more love and happiness than you have ever felt before. You will feel more serenity and contentment, and ultimately nothing will ever be congested inside you again.

Trust and believe you can attain a state in which you never have any more distress, turbulence, or chaos for the rest of your time on gravitational spaceship Earth. You *must* understand that life is giving you a gift, and that gift is the rhythmic current of events that commences at your birth and transitions with your death. These events are challenging, stimulating, and inspire great growth. To happily handle this rhythmic current of life, your heart and soul *must* remain open and expansive enough to encompass reality. The only reason they're not is because you react and resist. Learn and relearn to cease all resistance to reality, and what used to appear distressing will begin to appear as stepping stones on your spiritual voyage. No one is forcing you to relax, release, and let go of your misery. It is an option, too, though it's not necessary.

FEAR

There is a silent but deadly thing called adopted passive illusions. It is when we permit popular culture to name for us. It refrigerates our clarity in definitively knowing for ourselves a clear vision of what we desire for our lives. The fact of the matter is that happiness is very specific, not generic. And specificity pays handsomely. When you are specific about what things you desire from life, you must actively choose them, plan for them, and personally allocate resources on their behalf. We must intentionally work towards them so they will manifest.

We have made decisions and taken actions based on well thought out and intuitively based resolves leading to activities in our lives that give us joy, keep us sane and well maintained. Fear is taking your negative ***energy*** and cycling and depositing it into the hearts and minds of those closest to you. This poisons relationships: intimate, personal, and professional.

Present day is ripe for fear as now everyone is willing to sacrifice everything of value, like the power of love for the love of power, to have security and feel safe (the what if). Being free is no longer desired; it is safety. Life has become "me, my, I." “They" want what I have, so I must defend me and my fear. Ultimately your life becomes a struggle, you struggle with everything and everyone, either internally or externally, but usually both as one is a reflection of the other. You can begin to question this and change.

Can it be that when you stop blaming and shaming others you can fall into self-blame-shame based on past ghost patterns of ***energy,*** creating new terrains for struggling? Certainly, this is all our egos searching for victory by creating struggles, demanding quick results rather than appreciating the vibe and the view of the process. Focusing on how things get done rather than the quality and beauty in the process of how things get done.

As a result of this and past trauma you relinquish parts of your infinitely creative self. Once these passages are reclaimed and aligned, you stroll in the world more vibrantly, prancing in the flow of love and happiness more alive than ever before. You have broader and deeper experiences internally and externally. It is likened to swimming in the deeper force that makes the waves roll ashore. Our relationship with this intensely beautiful force can be as intense and personal as we desire.

Because we are not taught to deal with fear objectively (essentially, we are taught fear, we actually live in a society which promotes and feeds on fear), we subsequently hold on to fear. Since we do have fear, there are two ways to deal with fear: acknowledge it for what it is and let it pass through, or hold on to it and deny that it is there.

No one questions this. We all know we're doing it: building desirable and undesirable outcomes of "this person should...then I'll be okay." We work from the premise that we are to figure out how life is supposed to be, and then make it that way. No. Life is life. Dive in and swim. Only someone who looks deeper, and questions why we need the events of life to be a particular way, will question this assumption.

Where and how did we come up with this notion that life is not acceptable just the way life is, or that it will not be acceptable the way it shall be? Who said that the way life organically develops is not all right? Fear says so.

Just make a decision to cease struggling, cease fighting. Adversity means we are resisting. Resisting causes tension and fighting, struggling feeds on that ***energy*** of resistance while stunting growth—not to mention ailments of a garden variety, and these cause more tension and stress. Water has no adversity. It flows around, over, through, into and out of. Become like water. Let the fear out. Let it go. Let it flow away. When we let go, we drift along with the flow of events as they emerge, knowing the appropriate direction in the moment, but not warping and manipulating events into a master plan. Our life is spontaneous, and we cease spending ***energy*** on anger, frustration, and fear.

This may seem irresponsible, but it is far from irresponsible. In reality, relaxing, releasing, and letting go improves your capacity to respond positively in any given moment. Thus, constant transformation is available. You can look deep inside and make a conscious decision that you do not want your weakest link dominating your life. Freedom means talking to people because we find them interesting, not because we're afraid, lonely, insecure, or vulnerable. We want to have relationships with people because we genuinely like them, not because we need for them to like us. We want to love because we truly love, not because we need to avoid our internal erections and complications.

I hear you asking: how do we free ourselves? We free ourselves by finding ourselves. We are not the pain, fear, or loneliness we feel, nor are we the part that episodically stresses out. None of these intrusions have anything to do with us. We are the one who observes these things. Because our consciousness is separate and aware of these things, we can liberate ourselves. To liberate ourselves of our internal fears, we simply stop erecting, engaging, and interacting with them. The more we touch them, the more we aggravate them. Because we're always doing something to avoid feeling them, they are not allowed to organically work themselves out. If we desire, we can simply invite the intrusions to surface, and we can relax, release, and let go of them. Since our inner fears are simply congested ***energies*** from the past, they can be unanchored and liberated. The difficulty is, we either absolutely avoid situations that can cause them to surface and release, or we cram them back down under the guise of defending ourselves.

In this fashion, the stored ***energy*** from the past can be released from the heart and with them the thoughts which generate them. When they surface, there are many ways in which our reactions surface: eating, calling someone, or doing something else to quiet it down. Once you become aware of your personal reaction(s), instead begin to notice that you noticed. The one who observes this is you, the subject. What you are observing is the object. A feeling of fear, loneliness, or emptiness is an object, it is something you feel. But who feels it? You can separate reality from projections about reality. Your way through, up, and out is to just observe who is observing. It's really this simple. The one who observes is already unanchored. When you desire to be free of these ***energies***, you must let them pass through you instead of burying them deep inside you.

We can experience these feelings; they are just part of the nature of being human. Our body's sensory information receives our environment through pressure baroreceptors and thermoreceptors on our skin, light in our eyes, molecules on the chemoreceptors on our tongues and in our noses, or change in our cellular ensemble of tissues. Be open, become more conscious, and understand that you are in there and you have a highly sensitive part in there, too. Simply remain open, and begin to observe that sensitive part of you feeling intrusions. Observe it feel need, jealousy, anger, fear, et cetera.

Many great works of art have come to us from people who were in turmoil. It comes from the deepest part of one's being. We can encounter these rich human states without acting out, getting lost in them, or resisting them. You can remain open and observe that you observe and just examine how encountering loneliness or fear affects you.

- Does your posture change?
- Do you breathe slower or faster?
- Do you hold your breath?
- Does your body temperature change? How?

- What goes on when fear or loneliness is given the space it needs to pass through you?

Become an adventurer. Behold it and then it will disperse. If you don't get involved in it, the encounter will soon pass through, and something else will emerge. Just enjoy all of it. If you can do this, you will be unanchored, and the world of vibrant ***energy*** will open up a new depth within you.

Fear, loneliness, et cetera are not gotten rid of, you just cease to be engaged with it. It's just another object in the universe, like cars, grass, people, et cetera. It's none of your business. Just relax, release, and let go. That's what the Self does. Awareness does not struggle; awareness lets go. Awareness is simply aware while everything in the universe cascades before it.

Begin to cultivate a pure love and happiness for yourself, for the wholeness of your body, mind, and soul. Change can be viewed as wonderful.

- What is your personal goal in this life?
- Will your actions today be directed toward your life's goal?

Awareness exercises our listening muscles, our paying attention muscles, and putting on our listening ears. Listening is sacred attention. Make contact with reality in an unmediated fashion by observing and listening both to your internal and external environs.

By Self-sitting you begin to feel an ***energy*** that you have never encountered before. It comes up from the background, rather than the foreground, where you encounter your mind and emotions. Feel this flow of

energy surging up from deep within.

Waiting is an Action

- Why is heartfelt pain in any of your requests being delayed?
- How does this generate pain and/or fear?
- What is that feeling? Why is that happening?
- How can these meaningless things cause pain?
- What kind of life is that?
- What would life be like was it not dominated by pain and/or fear?
- Do you truly desire to carry that inside and have to manipulate the environment to avoid feeling it?
- Do you have any idea how many things can cause pain and congestion?
- Why do you want to be anchored in bondage to the pain of fear?
- If you don't want the pain of fear, why do you build a defensive encampment for it to be kept in?

Remember, the more intense and deep the resistance, the greater the power. Power is ***energy.*** Relax and release into it.

Here is an example of an addict-alcoholic control mentality: Someone says that thing is hot. Their minds immediately ask how hot is it? How painful is it? Thus they dive in where instinctively non addicts-alcoholics pull away, withdraw, or pull back to defend themselves from the heat of the object. The addict-alcoholic sees it as a challenge—a force to be reckoned with. Then they build a mental defense against the collection of stored pain. Their minds are on task constantly.

- What kind of life are you going to have filled with uneasiness, fear, and worry?
- Worrying about yourself is a mode of suffering, and how do you relieve it?
- How do you stop impatience, intolerance, and fear?
- Do you think that resistance will make the pain of fear disappear?
- Do you think you can control it?

Decode how to get rid of this pain, not make it over. When you desire to be free from the pain of fear ask yourself:

- What do I truly desire for my life?
- Why do I allow fear or anything or anyone to live rent-free inside of me?
- Do I actually think by doing an external makeover, the pain of fear will magically go away?

You *must* learn to cultivate desire and devotion instead of fear and pain every day because buried, too, is phenomenal beauty, love, and joy.

Trust me, on the other side of any pain and fear is ecstasy. Your innate greatness is concealed on the far side of any deep-seated fear and pain. It might feel hot inside as the pain of fear passes through. Embrace the heat in your heart. When you relax, fire purifies as does tears. That is the pain of fear being purified. Learn to enjoy this process. Tears are our friend just like water.

Spiritual growth becomes your reality when you willingly pay the price of admission and live openly. Be willing at all times, in all situations, to remain clear in the face of pain and fear, and work with your heart by relaxing and releasing into it like a moderate breeze. You will have your troughs and peaks like everyone else. But spiritual living is remaining in love and happiness regardless. You are living in your Power: the presence of God within you. Power is the flow of love and happiness.

Remember beyond phones, internet, radio and television connections is the most powerful connection that exists—the bond within. So get up, over, and beyond.

- Have you ever built your whole world predicated upon another person's behavior or the durability of a personal or professional relationship? Or a specific outcome?
- If so, have you ever had that foundation pulled out from under you?
- Somebody leaves you. Somebody dies. A pandemic strikes and something goes wrong, then what?

To grow, you tumble and fold into the motion and begin again: born again. This is one of the most important lessons of my life marked by disorientation, discomfort, and great evolution and growth.

If you truly want to see why you do things, cease doing them and observe what happens.

Why do we smoke, overeat, shop, judge, et cetera? Each instance, each act is saying, "Let me out of here!"

Would you like to go beyond? Would you like to feel no edges, likened to strolling on the clothing optional beach? No complaining, no wincing, no whining.

FACING, TRACING, AND ERASING Example B

Cycling is in a category apart from driving a car or even running. I am a slow, careful rider, hesitating at speeds over 20 miles per hour; but even so, there's a pleasure not just in the unaccustomed speed of motion, the ease with which a bicycle bends into and emerges from corners, but in the blending of so much sensorial information, spatial as well as visual. You become one with a bike in a way that's impossible in a car and unnecessary on a run.

While competing in a Duathlon event, out of nowhere a fear of cycling gripped me from my shoulders through my heart. This residual fear was from my prepubescent years: once, while riding a country lane in late Fall, a forest flanked the course, its branches forming a dark canopy overhead. I wasn't so much riding as soaring through a tunnel of green, a song dancing in my head under the helmet, the road unspooling ahead of me. The air felt liquid as I leaned left and right into the corners, appreciating in my sense of balance, and in the shifting weight across my muscles and joints, how my body and my bike worked the course.

Through an aperture in the trees ahead, I glimpsed the stone parapet of a bridge: the road was about to take a sharp turn. I slowed the bike for the turn, noting a glaze of surface green—moss on the tarmac—where the road emerged into sunlight. Abruptly the whole world shifted sideways: the back wheel had hit the moss and gone into a skid.

I was bearing down on the stone parapet at 20 miles per hour, out of control. Braking hard would worsen the skid, but the stone wall was thirty yards away, then twenty, fifteen, and I slipped off the road's camber and bumped along on rubble. I was trying to keep my eyes fixed on the road edge rather than on the river and its boulders below when the back wheel found purchase and, with a wriggle and swerve, I pulled up and caught the tarmac, then swerved over the bridge.

The entire world shifted and twisted sideways is how it felt: a momentary skid, over in a second, barely worth remarking on. But if it wasn't for the efficiency and accuracy of my sense of balance, I would have been killed.

Cycling that Duathlon course, as the embedded fear gushed through me, I prayed and pedaled, and pedaled and prayed. While focusing on the course, at once a heated and cool like breeze drifted through my heart as I breathed deeper, relaxed, and let go. After the race, in which I medaled, I cried a minimum of three times. Later, I went to a scheduled deep tissue and hot rocks massage with Kato, my favorite masseur.

During the massage Kato said, "It's okay. You can let go. I keep a bucket under the table just for that purpose."

Prior to his comment, internally I felt my entire upper body trying to release and my breathing was somehow semi-trapped and all I could do was breathe harder and listen to the music. Then post more intense manipulations and focused breaths, soddened, I let go with a loud moan—my body just moved into another space. All the misalignments from the cervical spine to the coccyx just felt realigned and opened. I could then feel each breath freely travel the distance through my entire body like never before. I laughed and I know Kato's letting go bucket was filled to the rim. Kato knew it as well.

Creatively, he said, "Someone outside this door just ran upstairs and said they'd have exactly what she was having."

Both the event and the massage physiologically and spiritually catapulted us to an entirely new level—a fifth dimensional space of having our ***energy*** more fully available in the flow of life—a phenomenal momentum of more positive actions, attitudes, and thoughts.

The self has been divided into emotional, physical, spiritual, and mental, but the truth is there are only two: physiological and spiritual, and all the others are under either one or the other. The two makes the whole. At once that Duathlon and the massage increased a consciousness of how control and fear lived in my deltoids, trapezius, and glutei as a final lunging place when the former two are filled to capacity, and how breathing is so attached to posture. The ecstasy of the event and all evolution and growth are mellowing. No more holding a ghost in crowds.

You will end up loving the edges because they point the way. Constantly relax and lean into them. Especially when you are dancing, lean into the discomfort, for it is just your body both recruiting and building unused pathways and muscles.

How We Overcome Fear

We control events, and events control us internally. Happiness is not an exercise; it is a state of mind. Culture attempts and assumes to determine milestones of happiness. This immediately takes us from an internal state to compare with things externally. Again to compare is to despair. Competition is an inferior gauge for happiness. Honor and celebrate your uniqueness.

The secret to your happiness and your freedom is to decide that suffering is optional and you do not want it residing in your life. Pain will come and pass through intermittently: this is inevitable with relationships and the process of growing, living, and learning. Well-being: vitality and health has no stress, fear, or psychic pain. Comparison creates the load of "am I good enough?" which is laden with fear, anxiety, self-consciousness, and insecurity. This creates a schism between your self-worth-value and access to the ***energy*** of love.

We are controlled by things externally, and these external things we try to control. Control is a heavy form of resistance. It creates tremendous pain all the time. Why do we carry on this way? Just enjoy living and being your best self every day. It is truly a wonderful state when you have processed all your pain and thereby your fears. It's a smile that radiates from your chest through your shoulders, meandering through your sternocleido-mastoids and downward, pushing up on your mandible to dance upon your facial muscles. The smile shown outward is **energetically** felt and can be seen without a mirror. It pulsates through your brain, down your brain stem and courses through your spine so that even your coccygeal plexus is awakened and **energetic**.

Mine was experiencing the death of a parent at a very young age. The overwhelming sense of abandonment lurked, and thus became the fear of someone dying that I loved. So I would only permit love in on a faraway level until the relationship with my ex-fiancé. My relaxing and subsequent release came with honestly admitting that I deeply resented death. I made peace with that truth, and made amends with death. I know, how does one make an amends with death? Fact: only living in love so deeply and loving another completely eradicated that pain and its unreasonable fear. Free from the past means free at last.

I was essentially attempting to build enough ***energy*** up to brace myself against ever feeling that kind of loss again. And to do that is impossible without abandoning the ***energy*** of being happy and free in the present. It was like being curled up in a living cocoon of negativity, waiting for death—my death—and I was prepared. I convinced my brilliant brain to take on this task and it did. That was its best solution: one of defended pain and fear of the future. In essence, the memory of the pain's ***energy*** locked, unreleased, and fully loaded, was killing me. Fundamentally, it was siphoning my vitality and wealth of health to live a living death. It seems illogical. But internally it was a reality until I grew through to the why, when, and how. Today, the pain of love is not a problem. It is worth the ride to live openly in love through water, through fire, or plain ordinary days!

When we are continually willing to go beyond our selves, limitation ceases. Spiritual freedom means you never give up. There is always a beyond. No complaining. No wincing. No whining. We are simply thoughts, emotions, and ***energy***—minor and major ***energy*** shifts.

- What are you holding on to?
- Why are you holding on?
- Is it pleasurable in some perverse fashion?
- How does this enhance your life?

The power of awareness, as the gateway of waking consciousness, ends up holding the object stable simply by concentrating on it. Just as objects can pass through water but not ice, which is simply concentrated water. As ice expands, so mental and emotional ***energy*** patterns become motionless and more penetrating when they experience concentrated awareness. The very action of segregating the amount of awareness focused on one particular object over another creates adherence. And the result of adherence is that selective emotions and thoughts remain in one place long enough to become the cornerstone of the mind. Adherence creates the bricks and mortar with which you erect a conceptual self. In the midst of vast internal space, using nothing but the suspension of thoughts, you create an arrangement of apparent resistance to rest upon.

- Who are you that is confused and attempting to erect a concept of yourself in order to be clarified?

This question represents the essence of spirituality. You will never find yourself in what you have erected to define yourself. You are the one who's doing the erecting. You may construct the most remarkable collection of emotions and thoughts—you may erect a truly amazing, incredible, and dynamic arrangement—but, obviously, it is not you. You are the one who was adrift, frightened, and confused because you focused your powerful consciousness away from your consciousness of Self. In this fear, in this pain, in the drifted state, you learned to adhere and retain the emotions and thoughts that were passing through your foreground. You used them to erect a personality, your **OJEC** base, a self-concept that would let you define yourself. Consciousness rested itself on the objects it was aware of and called it home plate.

Some examples: locked in a cage...I am a woman...I am a son...I am a certain age... I believe in God, or I don't believe in God. You are neither male nor female. You are consciousness which hears the thought and sees a woman or a man's body in the mirror.

Maintain your power. Most events in our lives are self-initiated. Events are neither good nor bad, not in themselves, but based on your reactions to them. You have to choose. You can make a highly complex relational arrangement out of them, and then present that compendium as who you are. But it is not who you are. It is just thoughts you have gathered around yourself in an attempt to define yourself. You do this because you are adrift inside. Basically, you attempt to erect a sense of stability and control in a constantly changing internal environment. This generates a bogus, but embraced, sense of security.

- Who have you ever permitted directly into your true inner self without the defense of your mental buffer?
- There is the work personality and the family personality—they are equal façades—but what about you, the one who is continuing the façades?
- It's not that there is anything inherently immoral with this. Obviously, everybody does it. But who are you that is doing this, and more importantly, why are you doing this?

It is imperative to comprehend that it's not just up to you what thoughts you adhere to and what persona you erect. Polity has a lot to say about this. There are acceptable and unacceptable societal actions for virtually everything: How to sit, how to work, how to speak, how to think, and how to feel about things, or more so, how not to feel about things. How does our polity brand these mental and emotional elements within us?

When you do it well, you are rewarded with hugs and showered with positive accolades. When you do not do it well, you are punished, whether mentally, physically, or emotionally.

Just think about how nice you are to people when they behave in accordance with your expectations. Now think about how you withdraw your love and retreat from them when they don't. This is not to mention getting angry or even violent (wars are a great example) toward them (beating, slashing children).

- What are you doing? You are attempting to change someone's actions by leaving impressions on their mind. You are trying to alter their collection of emotions, beliefs, and thoughts so that the next time they act, it is in the manner you expect.
- In truth we are all doing this to each other every day. Why do we let this happen to us?
- Why do we care so much whether other people accept the façades we put out there?
- Is it money?

Thus, it comes down to **why** we are adhering to our self-concept. If you stop adhering, liken an addict giving up their addictive substance, you will see **why** the inclination to adhere was there. When you let go of your façade and do not try to trade it in for a new one, your emotions and thoughts will become detached and begin moving through you. NICE! It will be a very alarming encounter. You will feel fear deep inside, and you will *be unable to get your bearings.*

This is what people feel when something very important externally does not fit their internal expectations. Like when someone calls you a b---- because you do not do what they expect. The façade ceases to work and starts to crumble. When it can no longer defend you, you encounter great fear and anxiety. If this were a script or story, this is when the victim offers the villain money and queries, "Is there something I can give you?"

And of course the answer is, "NO." However, you shall find that when you are willing to face that sense of fear, there is a channel through it. You can go further into the background of your awareness that is encountering it, and the fear will cease. Then there will be an immeasurable serenity, like nothing you've experienced.

This is the point very few people come to know: it can cease. The noise, the fear, the pain of confusion, the constant changing of these internal ***energies***—it can all cease. You thought you had to defend yourself, so you gripped on to people or things that were coming at you and used them to hide in plain sight. You took what you could get your gripping hands on, and you began to adhere in order to erect resistance.

But you can let go of what you're adhering to and begin to play a new sport. Remind yourself that relaxing, releasing, and letting go is a practice and a process, and it means to begin relaxing and releasing your defensive, obsessive emotional, physical, and mental adhesions. You just have to take the risk of letting it all go (I did it back in the nineties) and bravely confront the fear of pain that was propelling you. Then, and only then, you'll have a new passage through that part of you, and it will all be over. It will cease—no more straining or distress, just serenity. We take risks every day: eating red meat, crossing the street, driving, investing in the stock market, and getting out of bed in the morning.

Thus, any pain and fear of inner growth intervals can be accepted, rather than regarding them as life-threatening encounters to be avoided. From this space, with practice, decide to be in the flow of life as a person who has no enemies, as a person who cannot be harmed, as one who lives in love and happiness.

This voyage is a passage through that part of you where you have been straining to avoid. On your passage through that space of *stormy* instability, the awareness itself is your solitary relaxation. You will just be conscious that incredible realignments are happening. You will be conscious that there is no resistance. Only flexibility and mobility, like storm clouds passing through. And you will be at ease with that. You will be conscious that each moment of each day is evolving and you neither have control nor desire it. You have no expectations, no delusions, no perceptions, and no security.

You have ceased erecting a mental expectation of what's happening, but life is happening just the same. You are wholly content just being conscious of it. Here comes this moment, and it is full, then the next moment, and then the next. But that's truly what always happened.

Since we live in time, it is nearly impossible for our finite mind to comprehend that eternity is not a time concept, that it has nothing to do with the passage of time. Time, like all of us, is multifaceted and contradictory and full of oddities and surprises. Minute by minute, tick tock, tick tock...moment after moment has been passing in the foreground of your awareness. The difference is that in the immediate present you are able to see it happening. You see that your mind and your emotions are responding to these moments that are coming through, and you are doing nothing to stop it. You're doing nothing to resist or control it. You're just letting life evolve, both internally and externally.

When you take this expedition, you will get to the space in which you see exactly how the evolving moments bring up a sense of fear and pain. From the state of clarity, you will be able to encounter the powerful inclination to defend yourself. This inclination exists because you truly have no control, and that is disconcerting to you. But when you truly desire to develop more spiritually, you have to be willing to just observe the fear of pain without defending yourself from it. You must be willing to observe that this need to defend yourself is exactly where the full personality originated from. It was erected by creating an emotional and mental arrangement to escape from that sense of pain and fear. You are now standing unflinchingly with the taproot of the mind—the problem.

When you go deep enough, you can watch your mind being erected. You will observe that you are in the center of nowhere, in a vacuum of infinite space, and these internal objects are streaming toward you: emotions, thoughts and the images of worldly encounters are all flowing into your awareness. You will clearly observe the inclination to defend yourself from this stream by getting it under your control. There is a tremendously intense inclination to tilt forward and snatch selective images of people, places, and things as they stream past. You will observe that when you focus on these mental transmissions, they become elements of a complex arrangement where none exist.

You will observe events that took place ten, forty, fifty years ago that you're still holding onto. You will observe that you're literally seizing all your memories and collecting them in an orderly fashion, and saying that is who you are; that is what happened to you. But you are not those events. How can you define yourself as the things that happened to you? You were conscious of your existence before they happened. You are the one who is in there doing all this and encountering all this. You do not have to adhere to your encounters in the name of erecting a self. This is a forged self you are erecting internally. It is just an impression of yourself that you use as a shield.

Begin to practice not comparing yourself to others or to your previous spiritual experiences. You are not the same person. Those experiences are important but they happened to someone else a long time ago. Manifest a willingness to create new occasions for increasing your spiritual powers and expanding your consciousness.

Challenging the Final Mind Management Barriers

How long have you been shielded in there straining to keep it together? Anytime anything goes awry in the protective arrangement you created about yourself, you shield and justify reconstructing it. Your brain does not cease its mental torture of restless irritability until you've processed the event or somehow made it fade away. People feel their very existence is at stake, and they will struggle, argue, and fight until they regain control. This is all because we have endeavored to erect resistance where none exist. Now we have to struggle to maintain it. The problem is: there is no way out that way. So surrender, become like water, become totally nonresistant. It flows around, over and through things.

Surrender and remember your mind has filtered all your senses. Resolve to let go all presumptions. Make a decision to surrender the known and plummet into the unknown, accepting uncertainty as a new lover you have a lustful interest in. Chase it, follow it. Envision how it would feel, stroke it, fondle it. Surrender all your past inclinations and their ghosts, and make a promise to follow spiritual guidance, intuition wherever it leads. Endeavor to surrender and observe people, places, and things in fresh new colors like a young child!

Keep in mind there is no peace and there is no victory in straining and struggling. You were told not to create the foundation of your house on sand. Well, this is the ultimate sand. In truth, you created your foundation in a vacuum. If you persist in adhering to what you created, you will persistently and perpetually defend yourself. You will have to keep everybody and everything straight in order to reconcile your conceptual arrangement with reality. It's a constant strain and a struggle.

What it means to live spiritually is to cease participation in this strain and struggle. It means that the events that happen in the moment belong to the moment. They do not belong to you. You *must* cease defining yourself in relationship to them, and just let things ebb and flow. If an event happens that doesn't fit your conceptual arrangement, and you see yourself straining, struggling, and justifying to make it fit, just observe what you're doing. An event in the universe did not match your arrangement, and it's causing congestion inside of you. If you will simply observe this, you will find that it is actually shattering your arrangement. You'll grow to a point where you enjoy this because you have outgrown your arrangement. You'll define this as beneficial because you are no longer willing to invest any ***energy*** into erecting and maintaining your façade. Like being in water, just flow and float. Instead, you will actually allow the people, places, and things that disrupt your arrangement to act as the storm to shatter it and unchain you. This is what it means to live spiritually. These storms are new beginnings.

When you become truly spiritual, you are absolutely different from everybody else. That which everybody else desires, you don't desire. That which everybody else resists, you totally accept. You desire your arrangement to erupt, and you honor the encounter when something happens that can cause congestion within you.

- Why should anything that anyone says or does cause you to get congested?

You are just on a gravitational spaceship, Earth. You are here on a working holiday for a specified period of time and then you are going to go home.

- How can you live all stressed-out over everything?

Don't do it. If anything can cause congestion internally, it means it hit your arrangement. It means it hit the forged part of you that you erected in order to control your own definition of reality. But if that arrangement is reality, why didn't observed reality fit? There's nothing you can construct inside your brain that can ever be considered reality.

You *must* learn to be relaxed with psychological congestion. If your brain becomes hyperactive, just watch it. If your heart starts to heat up, let it go through what it *must*. Strive to find that part of you that is capable of observing that your brain is hyperactive and that your heart is heating up. That part is your channel up and out. There is no way up and out through erecting this arrangement of yours. The only way to become unanchored internally is through the one who observes: the Self. The Self simply notices that the brain and emotions are collapsing, and that nothing is straining to maintain them.

Of course this will be painful. But this is what is called delicious pain. The reason you erected the entire mental arrangement was to escape the pain of fear. If you allow it to collapse, you're going to feel the pain of fear that you were denying when you erected it. You *must* be open and willing to feel the pain of fear.

It will hurt like never before. You may get out of bed after a sleepless night, pray, cry, yell and still don't feel any better. You may turn the volume way up as you listen to music so you won't hear your own thoughts. Your heart may feel torched. Then one day—date unknown—you wake up, look outside, and it's a beautiful, bright, sunshiny day. But if you were to lock yourself in a fortress because you were afraid to emerge, or take medications, you would have to confront that fear of pain if you ever desired to come into contact with a fuller existence. Your fortress would not be defending you, it would be confining you.

To be unanchored, truly free, and enjoy life, you must

come out. You have to surrender and pass through the cleansing process (storm, purification, water, tears) that frees you from your mind. You do this by simply observing the mind being the mind. The up and out is through consciousness. Cease defining the congested brain as a negative experience; just try relaxing in the background. When your brain is congested, *do not ask*, "What do I do about this?" Instead ask, "Who am I observing this congestion?"

With practice you will comprehend that the center from which you observe congestion is stable. If your center appears unstable, just observe who is observing the congestion. In time it will stop. You will then be capable of lunging into the deep background of your being while observing your brain and heart creating their last throes of turbulence. When you come to that point, you will appreciate what it means to be spiritual. Consciousness surpasses what it is conscious of. It is as distinct as the moonlight is from what it shines upon. You are consciousness, and you can liberate yourself from all of this by relaxing deep into the background.

When you desire enduring peace, enduring love and happiness, and enduring joy, you have to grow through to the other side of the internal turbulence. Turbulence is volatility. And volatility is nothing more than an organic pattern of growth that is cyclical in nature. You can live a life in which waves of love can surge inside of you whenever you desire. It is the true nature of your being. You simply have to go to the other side of the mind. You do that by relaxing, releasing, and letting go of your learnt inclination to adhere. You do it by not using your mind to erect resistance. Remember, like water, become totally nonresistant. It flows around, over, and through things. You just make a decision, with no reservations, to take the voyage by constantly relaxing, releasing, and letting go.

Without delay, the voyage becomes almost instantaneous. You will grow through the part of you that has always been the fear of pain and, you will watch how that part has always strained to be in control. When you don't nourish that part, just continue relaxing, releasing, and letting go, and refuse to let it adhere. Ultimately, you will be in the background of your resistance. This is not something you do; it is something that happens through you. So manifest the willingness to let go, and trust that everything is already circuitously done.

- Are you able to live as if you were living in a present that is already past, already consummated?
- What are you afraid of?
- Why?

Your only way out is being the observer. Simply keep relaxing, releasing and letting go by being conscious that you are conscious. If you pass through an interval of darkness, shadowy depression, just ask "Who is aware of the darkness and shadows?" That's how you pass through the different cycles of your internal growth. You *must* continue relaxing, releasing, and letting go, and remain conscious that you are still there. When you've released the darkened the shadowy mind, and you're no longer adhering to anyone or anything, you will come to a space wherein it will all open up as your background. You are conditioned to being conscious of people and things in your foreground. You in the immediate present become awakened to a universe in the background of your awareness.

It never seemed like there was anything in your background. Because you were so conditioned and focused on erecting your arrangement of the emotions and thoughts passing in your foreground, there was no consciousness of the limitless space internally. Posteriorly, there is an entire universe. You're just not considering that direction. If you're open and willing to relax, release and let go, you will cascade backwards, and it will open into an ocean of ***energy.*** You will become charged with radiance. You will become charged with a radiance that has no shadows or darkness, with a joyous peace that "passeth all understanding." You will then stroll through every moment of your daily life with the flow of this internal force sustaining you, nourishing you, and guiding you from very deep within. You will still have emotions, thoughts, and an idea of self-value-worth-efficacy soaring about in internal space, but they will be just a minor part of what you encounter. You will not identify with anything external to the sense of self.

Once you attain this condition, you will never have to have the pain of fear and anxiety about anyone or anything again. The Source of creation will produce creation, both internally and externally. You will glide in love, peace, and compassion in the background of it all, yet live in gratitude of it all. There is no need for resistance when you are at peace with the limitlessness of your true Being.

CHAPTER FOUR: MEDITATION, PRACTICE, AND SPIRITUALITY

THE RHYTHMS OF LOVE AND HAPPINESS

> There is nothing either good or bad, but thinking makes it so.
> —William Shakespeare, *Hamlet*

The greatest spiritual conduit is life itself. To begin with, you have to comprehend that you only have one choice in this life, and it's not about your profession, whom you want to marry, or whether you want to seek out a God. People have a tendency to stress themselves with so many choices. But in the end, you can toss it all out and just make one fundamental, basic decision:

- Do you want love and happiness, or do you not want love and happiness?

It's as simple as that. Once you make that choice, your voyage through this life becomes crystal clear. Most of us don't dare give ourselves that choice because we think it's not in our power. Some may say, "Well, unquestionably I want love and happiness, but my fiancé deserted me." In other words, they want love and happiness, but not if their fiancé deserts them. But that wasn't our question. The question was, "Do you want love and happiness or not?" If you make it that simple, you will see that it truly is in your power. Digressing from love and happiness is mainly because we have ingrained proclivities that get in the way.

For a second time, the question is simply, "Do you want love and happiness?" If your answer is truly yes, then say it without conditions. After all, what the question really means is

- Do you want love and happiness from today for the rest of your time on spaceship Earth, without reservations?

Well, if you said yes, it may happen that your fiancé changes his mind, or your child dies, or the stock market crashes. These events may happen between now and the end of your life. But if you want to stay on the greatest spiritual voyage, then when you answer yes to that question, you *must* truly be sincere. There are no ifs, ands, or buts about it. It's not a question of whether your love and happiness is within your power. With absolute certainty it's within your power. It's just that you don't truly mean it when you say you are open and willing to remain in love and happy. Remember without **O**bligations, **J**udgments, **E**xpectations, **C**onditions. Any condition you manifest will restrict your love and happiness. You truly are not going to be able to manipulate people, places, and things and keep them the way you want them.

You have to give an unconditional answer. When my fiancé asked, "Will you marry me?" I said, "Yes." But he had a timeline condition on it. My yes was an unconditional surrender to love. But he withdrew. He no longer wanted to get married. If you decide that you're going to live in love happily from now on for the rest of your life, you will not only be in love and happy, you will become enlightened. *Unconditional love and happiness is the greatest system there is*. You don't have to read any scriptures or learn Sanskrit. You don't have to renounce the world. You just have to truly mean it when you say that you chose to be in love and happy. And you have to mean it regardless of what happens. This is really a spiritual voyage, and it is the most constant and direct channel to Awakening as could possibly exist.

Once you make a decision that you want to live unconditionally in love and happiness, something unsurprisingly will occur that challenges you. This challenge to your commitment is exactly what stimulates spiritual growth. In reality, it is the unconditional aspect of your commitment that makes this the greatest voyage. It's truly simple. You *must* decide whether or not you will break your vow.

- Is your word bond?

When everything is going your way, it's easy to live in love and happiness. But the moment something challenging happens, it's not so easy. You tend to find yourself saying, "But I didn't know this was going to happen. I didn't think I'd lose my job. I didn't think COVID-19 would happen. I didn't think that somebody would spill hot coffee on me. I didn't think that somebody would stand up at my wedding and say they object."

- Are you truly open and willing to break your vow of unconditional love and happiness because these events occurred?

The possibility of things that might happen to us that we haven't even thought of is vast. The question is not whether they could happen. Things are definitely going to happen. The actual question is whether we desire to live in love and happiness regardless of what happens. *The purpose of our life is to enjoy, learn and grow from each experience.* We did not come to spaceship Earth to suffer. We are not helping anybody by living in misery. Apart from our philosophical beliefs, the fact remains that we were born and we are going to die. In the interval, we can choose whether or not we desire to appreciate the adventure. Events don't determine our love and happiness. We can be in love and happy just to be alive. We can live in love and happiness as all these events happen to us, and then be happy to lovingly let go and die. If we choose to live this way, our heart will be open, and our soul will be so free that we will soar to the heavens.

This expedition leads you to an absolute state of grace because any part of your being that might add any **OJEC** to your commitment to love and happiness has to be eradicated. If you desire to live in love, you *must* relax, release, and let go of the part of you that wants to produce controversy and dramas. This is the part that thinks there is a reason not to live in love and happiness. You *must* rise above the personal, and as you do, you will organically awaken to the higher frequencies of your being.

Ultimately, enjoying life's experiences is the only reasonable thing to do. You're here on spaceship Earth, and never once have you worried whether gravity would stop supporting you. So open up more, zoom out and look at the bigger picture, the history of the universe has been one of quiet, slow expansion over time. Since you're already here, make a decision to live in love and happiness while you're here. You're going to die anyhow. Things are going to happen anyhow. Anticipate change, don't be surprised or overexcited by it, and above all, don't panic. Why not be in love and happy? You improve nothing by being disturbed by life's events. Does it change the world?

No, you are just miserable. Trust and believe there is always going to be something that can disturb you, if you choose to let it.

As tough as that sounds, what's the benefit of not doing it? You may as well make it an adventure. What sense does it make to not make it an adventure? It doesn't change anything. Ultimately, if you remain in love and happiness, you triumph. Make that your resolve, and just remain in love regardless of what happens.

The secret to living in love and happiness is very simple. Begin by understanding your internal ***energies***. When you look inside, you will see that when you're in love and happy, your heart feels open, and the ***energy*** streams up inside of you. When you're miserable, your heart feels turned off, and no ***energy*** flows up inside. Everything happens from the inside out. So remain in love and happy; keep your heart open. Regardless of what happens, even when your fiancé changes his mind for a timeline or any other reason, or the stock market crashes, remain open.

There is no law that says you must turn off. You can choose to turn away from destructive ***energy*** patterns and toward the more holistic ***energy*** patterns of life, emotion, and thought. Simply tell yourself that regardless of what happens, you're going to remain open and positive. When you begin to turn off, simply question if you're truly open and willing to abandon your love and happiness? You can explore what it is internally that believes there is some value in negativity and closing. The slightest thing happens, and you are willing to abandon your love and happiness. You were having a beautiful day until something or someone crossed your path at the supermarket. It got you very upset and you remained that way the entire day.

- Why? Dare to ask yourself that question.
- Was it hurt pride, self-pity, envy, arrogance, self-righteousness, or resentment?
- What benefit or value came from allowing it to deteriorate your beautiful day?

There was no benefit, no value. If something or someone crossed your path, relax, release, and let go. Stay positive and open. If you truly desire it, you can.

When you embark upon this adventure of no **OJEC** and happiness, you will grow through each encounter. You will have to remain aware, balanced, and committed unconditionally. You will have to have perpetual vigilance, remain open and responsive to life. But nobody said that you can't do this. Remaining open and willing is what the spiritualists taught. They taught that God is love, God is ecstasy, and God is joy. If you stay open and willing enough, surges of holistic ***energy*** will fortify your heart. Spiritual practices are not an end in themselves. They produce prodigious results when you become deep-rooted and willing to remain open. When you learn to remain open continuously, extraordinary events will come to pass for you. You simply *must* not be negative and switch off.

Love and happiness is a state of mind. The secret is learning to discipline your brain and body enough so that it is unable to deceive you into thinking that this time there's intrinsic benefit and value in being negative and closing. If you fall, get back up. Remember if you can look up, you can think up. So get up brush off your gray matter, and go it again. You are human, this will happen. Therefore the second you begin to negatively turn off and defend yourself, rise. Just pick yourself up and reaffirm internally that you desire to remain open, and nothing is going to turn you around. Reaffirm that all you desire is to be at peace and to be grateful for life. You have no desire for your love and happiness to be based on the obligations, judgments, expectations, and conditions (**OJEC**) of other people's actions and reactions. It is challenging enough that your love and happiness is conditional upon your own thoughts, words, and actions. When you begin making it conditional upon other people's obligations, judgments, expectations, and conditions, you're creating severe stress. Remember this rhythmic training system provides a mode to be physically relaxed, emotionally calm, mentally focused, heart happy, and spiritually conscious. Since stress is the number one killer, an entire chapter is devoted to it.

Things are going to happen to you, and you're going to have the inclination to switch off. But you have the choice to give in to it or relax, release, and let it go. Your brain will tell you that it's not rational to remain open when those things happen. But you have limited time left on this gravitational spaceship Earth, and what's truly not reasonable is not to live an open, joyous life.

When you have difficulties, recall that training is a metaphor for living, and training and meditation are just the proactive practice of getting out of the way.

As we think, so we become

Give voice to this meditation

A Deep Silence

- Pay attention, use your senses to go deeply,

and savor each smell, each encounter, and each beverage. Then move on completely to the next. As when training or running, your pace is set one repetition at a time and one step at a time, respectively. You cannot replay the last repetition or go back and rerun the last quarter mile, you can only run the current one.

- Sit in your silence and listen as deeply as possible. Allow the external silence into your internal space. Allow this to be the jumping off place for the remainder of your day. Try and cultivate internal silence amid external busyness. Just practice nonresistance; embrace it as part of the surround.

In this fashion, combined training and meditation strengthens your body and your center of awareness so that you're consistently conscious enough to keep your heart open. You remain open by simply relaxing, releasing, and letting go of the inclination to shut down. You just breathe and relax your shoulders when your heart becomes tense. When you're nearing the end of the opened flow, although it's unnatural, begin to relax, release, and let go so the flow continues uninterrupted. You don't have to be externally radiant constantly; you're merely blissful internally. Instead of wincing, whining, and complaining, you're simply making an adventure of the various settings revealed.

Living in unconditional love and happiness is a great voyage and a great system because it solves everything. This system for living in unconditional love and happiness is valuable because what you're doing with your remaining time on gravitational spaceship Earth is now defined—you're relaxing, releasing, and letting go of the bondage of self so that you can remain in love and happy.

This system is great because it allows you to master the one thing you can master—your response. It allows you to avoid closing and fear by determining your response. The discipline is training you to observe that each event will appear different than the last time. So ask yourself:

- Is this an ***energy*** pattern I have observed before?
- How did I respond?

Instead of closing with fear, you can choose to take a deep breath, relax, release, and stick to the system. As far as your spirituality goes, you're going to grow astronomically. A person who really practices this every moment of every day will notice a purification of their emotions and thoughts. This is because they have ceased getting involved in the debris that surfaces. Their soul is going to awaken to a new happiness and freedom that is beyond human understanding. The voyage of this system is a design for daily living and it resolves your spiritual ***energy.*** The highest gift one can give to God is to be pleased with God's creation. God is ecstasy and is as high as it gets. If you want to be close to the Mother/Father Source, learn to be gratefully carefree. If you remain spontaneously centered and joyful and let nothing turn you around, you will find the Mother/Father Source. That's the miraculous part. Yes, you will find love and happiness, but that's nothing compared to what you're actually going to find.

Once you have passed through trial by fire, and you

have no reservations about relaxing, releasing, and letting go regardless, then the veils of the human psyche and heart will wane. You will stand unequivocally with what is out there because there is no longer a need for you. When you are done adventuring with the secular and finite, you will open to the everlasting and infinite. Then the words "love and happiness" cannot describe your state. That's where words like ecstasy, bliss, liberation, utopia and rapture come in. The joy becomes irresistible, and your cup runneth over. This is a beautifying voyage. Rejoice and live in love and happiness.

PART TWO:
A Functional Transformation

CHAPTER FIVE: CREATING A HEALTHY BODY FROM INSIDE OUT

"MENS SANA IN CORPORA SANO-- A HEALTHY MIND IN A HEALTHY BODY"

Work is love made visible. Keep working with love.
—Anonymous

Stress has already been touched on in this book, but some rough experiences have convinced us it is so important that it deserves special attention.

The body is one big tube of pressure and fluid which must be kept balanced. Stress can be defined as a force that deforms. When there is perpetual emotional, psychological, and physical stress, the higher levels of adrenaline and cortisol that your body's natural stress response releases are maintained, leading to a compromised immune system and more likelihood of physical ailment.

First, here is a look at some of the physiological shapes and colors excessive stress seems at times to arrive in:

high blood pressure
heart palpitations
headaches
loss of appetite
disturbed sleep patterns

excessive sweating
dry mouth
muscle tension
irritable bowel syndrome
breathing problems
overeating
nail biting

Combined with these, there may be psychological and spiritual changes: depression, rapid mood swings, memory loss, anger, confusion, irrational fears, and serious sexual troubles.

This incomplete list is one of the reasons clinical research has proven that stress is the number one killer. Exercise is a positive stress and is so vital and essential to our daily lives and state of health: emotionally, mentally and spiritually.

Stress is a derivation of the Latin word meaning "to be drawn tight." There are two distinct forms of stress. Eustress: a positive stress with a beneficial effect wherein endorphins are released. It is a motivating presence. Distress: a negative stress with a detrimental, agonal strain, both physiologically and psychologically.

The effects of distress—which include panic, lack of self-confidence, anxiety, and doubt—are such that stress is perpetually at the root of every state of ill health and affects every part of your body. Eustress enables you to meet challenges, to push yourself into new areas of understanding or experience through amplifying your awareness and focusing your concentration.

By being conscious of your physical, emotional, and mental response to various situations you can determine when you are becoming "drawn" and strained into a constricted—off—state and the effect it has on your entire being. If not, when this response becomes increasingly stressful so you are no longer capable of maintaining your equilibrium, then your body translates this as life-threatening and puts you on high intensity red alert. And this distress has such a wide-ranging effect it affects all eleven body systems.

The physical reaction prepares the body to respond to the stressor. Although the lymphatic system and the endocrine hormone system were explored in some detail in another section, it is so important since this preparation begins in the hypothalamus, a small part of the limbic system in the brain that deals with emotions and feelings. This area also monitors your nervous system, your digestion, heart rate, respiration, and blood pressure. The high intensity red alert causes the release of adrenaline, cortisol, and other hormones. These hormones shutdown the digestive system to conserve ***energy***, increase heart rate to increase ***energy***, suppress the sensation of feeling so you can be injured and keep fighting or running, and increase your rate of breathing. This is how the pain of fear, food, and addiction are so forcefully interwoven.

What happens to these systems when there is no fight or flight in which to release the ***energy*** accumulating internally? In your digestive system it can lead to ulcers or irritable bowel syndrome, which is linked to high stress levels, and you get diarrhea, constipation, or a loss of appetite. What exactly happens to the inclination to scream, to lash out, and to find release from the tension? Unhealthy intimate and personal relations, food and alcohol increases, and chronic mental fatigue leading to breakdown or depression. Physical changes can be hunched and tight shoulders and gait changes.

Ultimately, the actual cause of stress is not the external situations or circumstances. The actual cause is our perception of them—whether that is overpowering fear or challenging perception. It is also our perception of our capacity to cope, as when we feel we have too many demands and not enough time. And our perceptions habitually come from our internal belief system about life and living.

The greatest lesson we can learn from stress physiologically and emotionally is that distress truly diminishes performance rather than enhancing it. There is that far more effective space where you are both fully relaxed and absolutely alert together, as a truly relaxed state inspires great creativity and productivity. In a relaxed and released state we have access to immensely more physical and mental ***energy*** levels.

Through rhythmic training, we can work with our natural eustress response and develop a higher level of adaptability by changing our body, our perceptions, and our responses. Put the pieces together to transform your normal responses to reality, to embrace a deeper meaning, and to find peace and ease in the full enjoyment of living in love and happiness. When physiologically you're in this "stress" state your ability to reason and think logically is compromised, you're vulnerable to living fearful (flight) or aggressive (fight) decisions. In the limbic system or amygdala, decision making becomes extremely rapid, black-and-white, and fear driven. The terrified does whatever it thinks it needs to do to eliminate the perceived threat as hastily and efficiently as possible. It doesn't care about discipline or the long term; it just wants to feel safe again. That's why the limbic system *must* never be your spiritual advisor.

We can view our training and spiritual work as learning to live life without stress, disturbances, fear, or exaggeration. Even when things are not so good our physical ***energy*** is dynamic, never static. Using this voyage of life to evolve spiritually is absolutely the greatest system. With this system, we take what comes. The sunshine and rainbow, the high and low—it's a steadfast consciousness. There truly is no reason for tension and troubles. Stress only occurs when we resist life's events. When we're neither pushing life away nor pulling it towards us, then we are not generating any resistance. We are just present. In this state, we are simply observing and experiencing the event of life evolving. When we choose to live this way, we will observe that life can be lived in a state of serenity.

What a miraculous process life is, this flow of atoms through space and time. Since every person, place, and thing are currents of ***energy,*** living in this process can be a resolution. The universe is undergoing constant change and therefore we are at once interplaying at a distance and up close and personal. We are all sub processes of each other, in-between one event and another. When you embark upon this voyage, this system produces power to enter into living fully in the space and the contours of acceptance and serenity. It's simply an everlasting sequence of arrivals. If you resist this miraculous power of life, tension erects itself within you and inhabits your body, resulting in physiological, psychological, and spiritual heart imbalances.

It is not difficult to see the inclination toward resistance and stress in daily living. But when we desire to understand this inclination, we *must* first study why we are so resistant and stressed to just letting life be life. What resides inside of us that even has the capacity to resist the full enjoyment of simply living? When you look prudently inside yourself, you will observe that it is you, the Self, the indwelling being, which has the ability. It is called willpower.

Will is a real ***energy*** that emanates from our being. It is what makes our fingers and toes move. They just don't move erratically by themselves. They move the way they do because we assert will to make them do so. We use the same will to hold onto emotions and thoughts when we desire to focus on them. The power of Self, when it is focused and directed into the physical, psychological, or spiritual realms, creates a power, and we call that power "will." That's what we use when we seek to make things happen or not happen. We are not toothless, bald, and helpless in there; we possess the power to affect things.

CHAPTER SIX: UNDERSTANDING NUTRITION, EXERCISE, AND GOAL-MAKING

CHANGING, DANCING, AND EVOLVING

Let there be everywhere our voices,
our eyes, our thoughts, our love, our
actions, breathing hope and victory.
—Sonia Sanchez

THE RHYTHMIC TRAINING DANCE

Foundation Shade		2 Weeks	Black and White
Buildup Shade		3 Weeks	Pink
Strength Shade		4 Weeks	Orange
High Intensity Shade		4 Weeks	Blue
Maximum Strength		4 Weeks	Green
Recovery Transition Shade		2 Weeks	Purple
Maximum Fat Loss Shade		8 Weeks	Yellow
Transition Shade		1 Week	Red

The Rhythmic Training Dance is a system of maintaining mind, body, and soul from the deleterious effects of distress, struggling, and the pain of fear, as well as a natural method to keep the effects of aging and sarcopenia at a minimum. It encompasses an effective holistic strategy to groom, nourish, nurture and transform the emotional, mental, physical, and spiritual ***energies*** over 28 weeks; commencing with the first New Moon of Fall so that the intense training is during the holidays when over indulgence in fears, foods, and stress tends to be the norm.

This system will be even more powerful when you begin to combine it with the other implements. But, for now, let us look at the specifics of how the Rhythmic Training works.

Overview: Training Loads & Repetitions for Shade Goals

As Resistance training is the only natural stimulus that causes increases in lean tissue mass to any appreciable degree, the application of load and repetitions is the means by which your goals are accomplished. 1 Repetition Maximum (1RM) ranges are associated with these training goals. Relatively heavy loads are used when the goal of the shade is strength or power. Moderate loads for high intensity and light loads for transitions and muscular endurance and fat loss.

A certain RM emphasizes a specific outcome, but the training benefits are blended at any given RM since this method appears to be appropriate for assigning load and repetitions in a program, it means that testing is required and preferable to "guess work." You can either directly test your 1RM for an exercise, or you can perform a multiple RM test for the exercise.

Basically, understand that it is simply a certain percentage of the maximum amount of weight that can be lifted while maintaining proper form and technique for a single repetition. You can perform this by yourself, or you can have this done at your local gym for free. Just remember if machine exercises are being used, you will always be able to perform more repetitions at a given % of the 1RM compared to free weight exercises

Where Are You Beginning?

Progression, Overload, Specificity, Holistic Dieting, and Meditation is a recipe for physique harmony and beauty. Consistent, regular training and adherence to these basic principles helps you to reach and maintain your ultimate goal—a healthy mind in a healthy body (with rewarding milestones along the way). Each one of these principles is essential to an active, healthy system. Practiced just right, each can be a joy and a delight as they gently and very gradually infiltrate your life.

1. Start keeping a "diet training journal." Engage your physical motor system by writing down your milestones and your goal, and continue keeping a journal. Recall that the act of writing involves you physiologically as well as psychologically, thus adding even more power to your evolving training efforts.
2. Select a number from 1 to 28. Mark it down

on your calendar. This will be your Baby-Body Dieting Day. On this date every month, you may indulge in, and thoroughly *enjoy,* sweets of your choosing.

3. Write down every mouthful of food you normally consume and add up the calories, the carbohydrate calorie content, the protein calorie content, and the fat calorie content. Resist the urge to cheat because you are writing it down. Do this for three days. One must be a weekend day. Figure out how many you are ingesting. See it as a portrait—a metric picture of your physique!

4. Depending on your general condition and starting weight, a loss of from one to two pounds per week is a realistic goal to aim for. Greater loss is achievable but undesired. Keep in mind, there are structural factors to be considered in losing weight. Most importantly there is internal fat holding your abdominal organs in place. If you trim down too quickly, before you have had time to build up muscle tone to substitute for your fat, it can result in prolapsis (abdominal organs falling from their normal position). Recall that the contents of your abdomen include your abdominal muscles and parts of your digestive tract as well as parts of your diaphragm.

5. Record your weight. Numbers are factual. You will have these measurements to guide your progress. They can assist you in remaining focused on where you are, how far you have progressed, and each milestone along the way.

6. Take your chest, waist, hips, and thigh

measurements at least once a week. The optimal time to weigh and measure is first thing in the morning of each Lunar Cycle—New Moon, First Quarter, Full Moon, and the Last Quarter—before you ingest anything. Use the same scale. Always measure the parts at the exact spot and use the same amount of tension on the tape. Never cheat subconsciously. It is easy to let your zeal get the better of your accuracy. Be sure to use a measuring tape which is made of oilcloth-like material that will neither expand, nor contract, and is unaffected by dryness, wetness, cold, or heat.

7. You must have your body fat measured by a professional. Body fat calipers are the most accurate, and generally a trainer at a local gym will take it for free if you inquire. It is prudent to have the same person measure you every time, so try and stay in contact with that person. Identify where you are on the following table.

PHYSICAL CONDITION	**FEMALES % FAT**	**MALES % FAT**
Very Lean	<19	<9
Lean	19-22	10-14
Desirable	23-27	15-19
Average	28-35	20-25
Typical Unhealthy	>35	>25

Begin where you are, right here and right now!

- Beginners: Learn to dance between the

variables.

- Intermediates: We want to find the limit, converge at the edge and dance as close to it without touching from both sides.
- Advanced: Restraint of Tongue and Time.

If you never look at how you train, you never get to discover the power of that **energy**. "It's what you learn after you think you know it all that counts." In many ways, it can be different from what you previously believed about fear, diet, training, and **energy**; and so are you.

We know by rhythmically invoking the eleven body systems to express and sustain health, self-image, and -efficacy, your rhythmic training not only assists and helps to create self-image and -mastery, but it is in some important ways dependent upon *self-efficacy* as well. In the long run, what we are doing is trying to alter that image. Since body image, posture, and spirit are intimately connected and all three are shaped by experiences:

- What are you saying with your body, your mind, and your soul when you live in fear and resistance, when you tighten your chest, rounding your shoulders forward?
- When you ingest nutrient-deficient foods?

Going to another Shade or going for that extra repetition is just another way to deepen the experience. The blood flow changes, the tissue becomes firmer, increasing sensation, awareness is heightened, as is function, as is a piece of your health and *self-efficacy*.

There is something spiritual here! Let your **energy** run the process and dictate the progression. All of this is based on accepting your body's natural **energy**, design for fear-free thinking and movement, and rejuvenating powers. Your faith is your confidence that gives you room to breathe, maintain, and improve. This internally guided process completes itself in a healthy manner.

The working definition of **healthy**:

- Greets each day full of ***energy*** and vitality
- No headaches or pain in your body
- Capable of initiating and sustaining healthy coitus pleasure
- Has no need for drugs and chemicals
- Strong, graceful, firm, fear-free thinking and mobile body
- Sleeps soundly and restfully

Experience reveals that quality and quantity *must* go hand in hand. The only way to do anything healthy is to understand healthy. It is just that simple. Your support, your faith, and your *perseverance* create a space for this natural unfolding.

Remind yourself over and over again—day in and day out: It is the stacking up of the "additives," fear, and lack of training which eventually cause unhappiness and the almost unbearable burden of overloaded and degenerated joints, as well as the loss of fear-free thinking and mobility with fruitless and useless pains, strains, and canes.

MILESTONES, REWARDS, and CONTRACTS

Set up a reward at each transition. Construct a thoughtful, systematic motivational system. A systematic motivational reward is the golden key that opens the portal to your living The Rhythmic Training Dance. For example, it can be accomplishing a physical goal, fitting into a suit, sexy dress, or lingerie—the kind you have been unable to wear for many years, if ever. Register for the event or go out and purchase it—hang it up where you will constantly see it, and *with confidence,* anticipate the day when you can do or wear it.

Remember, successful dancing requires that you learn and systematically use the benefits of rewards. These are in addition to the **Inspirational Affirmations** built into your training. It must be ***fun!*** It must be some tangible reward—a day trip, an event, a new car—some reward that you will enjoy once you have achieved your physique health goal.

Create a self-contract. **Now!** For instance, "For every pound that I lose or fat percentage that I drop (or both), I will put twenty dollars into a fund toward the guilt-free purchase of that new________ that I desire to own, because I, your full name, shall sincerely deserve it!"

You must be specific about your actions and the reward entailed. Write it down—the weight you desire to achieve and the reward that awaits you when you reach your goal.

To further inspire you, post on your refrigerator, your screen savers, and your pantry cupboards, too—a picture of yourself when you were happier or slimmer. Remember that all the Training Dance Shades are on a day to day, shade to shade approach, and each shade needs to be rewarded. This is true regardless. You show up for each session in the shade so you deserve your contractual rewards along the way. This carries an added psychological lift knowing that the entire dance has had supplemental, externally enjoyable benefits for you, plus your spiritual and physiological outcome.

Start now, set your milestone, and begin. Remind yourself that the Rhythmic Training Dance can succeed only when the routines are actually completed; mere contemplation renders no results. Besides, once you begin applying your implements and new knowledge, you will actually enjoy dancing from shade to shade. Trust your dance.

METABOLISM

First, it is necessary for you to understand precisely what you are working with so you can understand what kind of changes you want to happen within your physique in order to achieve the visible changes you desire to happen on the outside. Second, hormones regulate your metabolism of carbohydrates, proteins, and fats. They function to increase the rate at which your cells release ***energy*** from carbohydrates, enhance protein production, and activate fats. They can be suppressed and serve to decrease that rate.

Quite simply, your basic metabolic rate is how many calories you need to sustain your current weight. And your metabolism is how many calories you expend in a typical day. It is affected and controlled by your thyroid and is primarily a factor of your lean muscle mass.

Men and women of various ages adapt to training in essentially the same ways. To lose fat you must expend more calories than you ingest and the keystone to accomplishing this is anaerobic work. Aerobic work only expends calories while performing it. Anaerobic work expends calories during performance and increases your caloric expenditure for hours post training. In regards to strength training, when you build muscle and sustain it, you expend more calories constantly—while working, resting, playing, and sleeping. During sleep nearly 100 percent of your ***energy*** expenditure comes from fats because of the very low intensity of the activity.

In this manner, increasing your metabolism is the keystone in long-term fat loss and changing your physique; however, in reality, metabolism is only one of the training components. It is the keystone, but without the other stones—fear-free thinking, balanced nutrition, and rest—to create the base and arms, keystone or no, there will be no triumphant arch to pass through to successful spiritual and physical maintenance and optimal health.

To reiterate, your strength training will expend more total calories, and more fat calories overall, than expended at lower intensities. Moreover, lean muscle is one of the biggest ***energy*** expenders of your body, so the more muscle you possess, the simpler it is to reduce fat.

Along these lines, your body's muscle tissue is the only tissue that "burns" fat. Aerobic work makes your muscles more efficient at expending fat. Subsequently, since your muscle tissue is the only tissue that "burns" fat, and aerobic work makes muscle smaller and more efficient at expending fat, then basically you are producing a smaller, more efficient fat expending physique. This is counterproductive.

As was stated previously, your metabolism is essentially a function of how much muscle your physique possesses. Since aerobic work neither builds nor maintains muscle, its contributions are null in raising your resting metabolism.

Thus, your body adapts to aerobic work by decreasing your metabolism and sanctioning your body to amass more fat. In that regard, without going into too much detail, anaerobic training also has a profound impact on caloric expenditure. First, it directly increases your need to "burn" calories to fuel your training, and it also raises caloric expenditure indirectly by increasing your muscle mass, because with strength training as you progress, you add more intensity or gradually increase the resistance.

WOMEN

Hormones trigger numerous physiological and psychological changes in a woman's physique, including but not limited to weight gain, mood swings, and water retention. It is well documented that these are exacerbated by nutrition deficiency, inadequate application of training, and in some, excessive physique weight. Across time, these choices can result in chronic health conditions, including osteoporosis, fatigue, negative abdominal adiposity, and decreased vigor and mental acuity.

Women who reliably train holistically as a lifestyle can maintain balance more efficiently through hormonal challenges and other life stressors, increase lean mass, improve lipid profiles, and sustain mental acuity. Such weight bearing exercises promote bone mineralization, which fights against osteoporosis. Bone responds to the amount and rate of external loading. Therefore strength training movements through your full range of motion are essential to sustain your tissue viability. Strength training is both effective and efficient for this task as it engages the systematic increase in weight and intensity through progressive overloading.

Furthermore, as women add years, their physiques are no longer built for reproduction, their metabolic rates and requirements decrease whilst their propensity for higher fat storage remains constant or increases. Thankfully, gaining muscle counterbalances this natural phenomena. Every pound of muscle added commands approximately 50 calories per day to sustain. Moreover, training and development of this muscle commands calories. Deliciously, this is about 5 pounds of fat or 18,250 calories per year for this muscle to simply lounge around accentuating your curves.

In this manner the Rhythmic Training Dance provides proper progression, variation, specificity, and overload for the successful stimulation and adaptations vitally important for your optimal physiological longevity. You must train with enough intensity to initiate and sustain your bone, muscle, cartilage, ligament, and tendon adaptations for mobility and postural balance as you add years.

Commit to memory that it is imperative for women to build and maintain the strength and flexibility of their abdomen, back, pelvis, and thighs. Meticulous strength training will greatly enhance your life–in coitus, moderating menstrual and menopausal discomfort, in childbearing, and sustaining your youthful contours over time. Therefore, practice squatting often as it engages the greater articulation of your ankles, knees, and hips.

Shapely hips and thighs are an attractive symbol of your distinct ***energy*** and power, and sexy has little to do with what you look like. It is how you feel about what you have to work with. How do you project your ***energy?***

Iron

It is well documented that women have particular iron requirements.

- To support in your absorption of iron, ingest foods rich in vitamin C at the same time you ingest the food containing iron. It is already contained in—and is more simply digested from—your vegetable and fruit sources (refer to the Outline Diet List).
- If you are taking an iron supplement and vitamin E, take them at a different time of day, as the iron supplement will tend to reduce the effect of the vitamin E.

Juicing is an excellent method for "pumping iron" requirements.

REGENERATOR

Use in order:
1 cup parsley
1 small Granny Smith apple
4 broccoli florets
3 celery stalks
½ lemon (with peel)

IRON SPRITZER

½ cup pomegranate (seeds only)
1 cup cherries or blueberries
1 small bunch of grapes
2 beets
¼ fennel bulb
⅓ cup parsley

Most Common Injuries

Essentially, strength training research has been growing dramatically, and gives further credibility to concepts that were for many years only anecdotal in nature. Yet, the design and practice of strength training regimens will never be led step by step with scientific studies. It is the combination of solid principles, practical insights, professional experiences, and directions based on scientific findings that result in the *optimal* knowledge for creating specific training regimens. The interlacing of the theory and science of teaching and leadership principles with the art of how to personalize these principles is critical to promoting a more sophisticated practice of strength training.

Due to the wide range of physiological variation, it is essential to educate participants to the effects of such training on their physique. The most common fear of many women is that strength training will make them look like a man. This can affect the quality of training if women are not completely comfortable with strength training because of fear. Without anabolic drugs there is little chance of women looking like men through strength training.

Another fear of women is sustaining injuries. There is absolutely no data indicating that women are generally more susceptible to weight training related injuries. However, statistically, there are a couple of factors that lead to injury. First, between 85 to 90 percent of all disc herniations occur at the lumbar spinal junctions. When the lumbar and thoracic spine is allowed to move into kyphosis, this sets the stage for possible vertebral disc injures. It has been shown that the muscles of the low back are capable of exerting considerably higher forces when the back is arched rather than rounded (kyphotic). Weakened abdominal and postural muscles increase spinal vulnerability to injury, as well as compromised breathing. Thus, we practice daily abdominal training.

More Planks No Spanx. Better To Maintain Than Regain.

The contents of your abdomen include your abdominal muscles, parts of your digestive tract, and parts of your diaphragm. However, the most abundant substance in your abdomen is fluid, and the majority of mass in your abdomen is water. Thus, when you contract your abdominal muscles forcefully during two foot barbell lifts, this pressurizes the fluids in your abdomen, and increased abdominal pressure significantly reduces the forces imposed on your spinal erector muscles and significantly reduces compressive forces on your discs. This is why abdominal strength is vital in spinal health and activities of daily living.

Accordingly, it is important to strengthen and maintain all the musculature enclosing your abdomen, hips and pelvis, anterior, and posterior for movement and postural balance. Abdominal strength protects your spine, pelvic floor, neck, shoulders, lower back, and hips. As a result, begin and continue to regulate your breathing and maintain your posture when stressed and fatigued, and improve the integrity of your neck and dècolletage while eliminating your postural weaknesses.

Creating Your Nutritional Proportions Base

As was stated previously, metabolism refers to the transfers of ***energy***. The ***energy*** released from your food—proteins, carbohydrates, and fats—transferred into the ***energy*** currency of your physique. Ingest five to seven smaller meals, as they are simpler to absorb and will enhance your metabolism. Each meal will consist of a protein, carbohydrate, and fat. Space them approximately 2.5 to 3.5 hours apart.

Caloric balance is important and nutrition is effectively covered in another section, but suffices to say that 1 gram of protein provides 4 calories, 1 gram of carbohydrate provides 4 calories, and 1 gram of fat provides 9 calories.

Protein has a high thermic effect of food, which means your body uses more calories to assimilate it than it uses with carbohydrate. So, by ingesting a higher percentage of your calories as protein can cause your body to expend more calories and assist in your fat loss. However, never forgo your ***energy***, as protein is rarely converted into ***energy***.

Optimum Protein Intake

Maintenance	**1.0 - 1.25 grams per pound body weight**
Maximum Fat Loss	1.25 - 1.50 grams per pound body weight

Caloric Expenditure

Calculate your basic daily ***energy*** requirement—your

basal metabolic rate (BMR). A modified Harris-Benedict formula is preferable.

Women

BMR = 655 + (9.6 x lean weight in kg) + (1.7 x height in cm) - (4.7 x age)

Men

BMR = 66 + (13.7 x lean weight in kg) + (5 x height in cm) - (6.8 x age)

Lean weight = (total body weight minus body fat percentage)

Conversions: pounds to kg multiply by 0.454

Inches to cm multiply by 2.54

EXAMPLE

A 55 year old woman weighing 152 lbs with 17.1% body fat equals a lean weight of 126lbs (57kg) on a 5'4" (163cm) frame:

BMR = 655 + (549.2) + (276.4) - 258.5

BMR = 1222 calories daily

Now that you know your BMR, you need an accurate activity level chosen based on the following:

Activity Level Factor	Activity Level
1.0	Sedentary (sleeping and watching television)
1.2	Very Light Activity (desk work with no physical activity)
1.4	Light Activity (desk work and above average walking)
1.6	Moderate Activity (desk work, above

	average walking, and a daily training routine)
1.8	High Activity (desk work, above average walking, and 2 daily training routines or physical work and a daily training routine)
2.0	Extreme Activity (Highly physical work plus intense daily training)

EXAMPLE

The amount of food required to maintain her current body weight at a high activity level (1.8)

BMR x 1.8

= 2199 calories to maintain her current weight

How to calculate your caloric expenditure percentages and protein requirements for each Shade of training:

Foundation Shade	**Maintenance x 120 - 125%**
Buildup Shade	Maintenance x 105 - 110%
Strength Shade	Maintenance x 115 - 117%
High Intensity Shade	Maintenance x 117 - 120%
Maximum Strength	Maintenance x 90 - 95%
Transition	Maintenance x 83 - 85%
Maximum Fat Loss Shade	Maintenance x 70 - 75%
Transition	Maintenance x 80 - 85%

EXAMPLE

She is currently in her Maximum Fat Loss Shade, and due to her high activity level, she will require her maintenance plus 70 to 75% to reach her goal:

Daily Calories = 2199 x 70 to 75%

Daily Calories = 1539 to 1649 calories daily

Protein Intake =152lbs x 1.25 to 1.5g per pound of body weight x 4 (calories in 1g of protein)

Protein Intake=760 to 912 calories

The remaining ***627 to 889 calories*** *can be distributed between her carbohydrates and fats.*

Remember that during any Maximum Fat Loss Shade, always increase your protein intake because if the rate of protein breakdown exceeds the rate of protein synthesis, you will lose muscle mass. However, this increased protein helps to preserve your muscles with your decreased carbohydrate intake.

SIMPLE HOLISTIC DIETING

- How and What, When and Why Digestion and Nutrition

  - Begin to avoid ingesting meat and high quantities of starchy carbohydrates at the same meal.
  - Stop combining too many foods at one meal. Your digestive enzyme activities differ for starchy carbohydrates and for proteins.
  - Cease ingesting refined sugar. It is a statistical fact that refined sugar is as

dangerous and addictive as heroin.

- Concede to the fact that cows' milk creates a tremendous amount of mucous and is difficult for your digestive system to process. Additionally, cows' milk is extremely constipating (healthy alternatives are on the outline diet list).
- If you must have cows' milk, have it in moderation—not too much. It needs to be unpasteurized, certified raw, and ingested alone. To prevent flatulence drink it slowly over a period of at least 5 minutes.
- Stop consuming your food hastily. Begin to masticate each mouthful for the process of digestion begins in your mouth. Allow your salivary glands to properly coat each mouthful by chewing at least 5 to 20 times. Practice!

Outline Diet List

Space does not permit an extensive discussion here of the vast amount of research carried out on the value of nutrition. In all probability, by now you are convinced and enthusiastic about enhancing your physique and your nutrition, as well as your *self-efficacy*.

Principally, this is a general dietary outline. The combinations can be altered and mixed to accommodate your preferences, but be certain you ingest the proper proportions to adequately supply your body's calcium, iron, and vitamin requirements.

- ❖ **Proteins**
  - Eggs/Omega 3 Eggs (7 grams per whole egg

and 3 grams per white)

- Lean Meats: Beef, Chicken and Turkey Breasts, Veal, and Lamb (20 grams per 3 ounces)
- Protein Powders (15-20 grams per scoop)
- Pollack (19 grams per 3 ounces)
- Tuna (18 grams per 3 ounces)
- Lump Crab Meat (17 grams per 3 ounces)
- Wild Caught Salmon (16 grams per 3 ounces)
- Raw Unpasteurized Cheese (7 grams per ounce)
- Low Fat Dairy Products (3 grams per ounce)
- Durum Wheat (14 grams per 4 ounces)
- Spelt (6 grams per 4 ounces)
- Wild Rice (4 grams per ounce)
- Rye (10 grams per 4 ounces)

- Legumes: Dried Beans- Edamame (10 grams per 4 ounces), Black or White (9 grams per 4 ounces), Pinto (9 grams per 4 ounces), Navy (8 grams per 4 ounces), Mung (7 grams per 4 ounces); Dried Peas- Black Eye or Cow (8 grams per 4 ounces), Chick (9 grams per 4 ounces), Pigeon (7 grams per 4 ounces), Split (8 grams per 4 ounces); and Lentils- Brown, Red, or Green (9 grams per 4 ounces).*

- Nuts: Peanuts (7 grams per ounce), Almonds* and Pistachios (6 grams per ounce), Cashews (5 grams per ounce), Pine Nuts* or Walnuts (4 grams per ounce).

- Seeds: Pumpkin*(8 grams per ounce), Sesame

(2 grams per Tbsp), Sunflower (5 grams per ounce).

*High Iron

- **Nondairy Milk Alternatives**
  - Almond, Cashew, Rice, Hemp, Hazelnut, and Coconut.
- **Starchy Carbohydrates**
  - Ezekiel Bread (18 grams per slice)
  - Rolled Oats Oatmeal (22 grams per 3 Tbsp)
  - Whole Wheat Pasta (42 grams per cup)
  - Whole Grain Bread (12 grams per slice)
  - Whole Wheat Bread (12 grams per slice)

- **Gluten-Free Starchy Carbohydrates**
  - Brown Rice (37 grams per cup)
  - Brown Rice Pasta (98 grams per cup)
  - Wild Rice (120 grams per cup)
  - Rye & Spelt Bread (25 grams per slice)
  - White Rice (40 grams per cup)
  - Corn (41 grams per cup)
  - Sweet potatoes, yams with skin (53 grams per 8 ounces)
  - White potatoes (51 grams per 8 ounces)
  - Brown Rice Cakes (7.3 grams per cake)
  - Carbonated Drinks (69 grams per 8 ounces)
- **Non-Starchy Carbohydrates (Vegetables)**
  - Amaranth*, Broccoli*, Brussels Sprouts*, Cucumbers (in season), Peas, Beans, Beets*, Peppers, Lentils*, Red/White Cabbage*, Onions*, Pumpkin*, Squash, Swiss Chard*, Carrots*, Turnip, Watercress, and Zucchini.

- **Non-Starchy and Sugarless Carbohydrates**
  - Lettuce, Celery*, Cauliflower, Asparagus*, Bok Choy*, String Beans, Kale*, Eggplant, Radishes, Cabbage*, Spinach*, Spirulina*, and all Greens.
- **Non-Starchy Carbohydrates (Fruits)**
  - Apples†, Avocado, Breadfruit, Berries* (Straw-, Blue-, Cran-, Black-, Boysen-, Goose-, Mul-, Logan-, and Rasp-), Melon (in season), Oranges‡, Bananas, Pineapple‡, Pomegranate, Lemon‡, Grapefruit‡, Papaya, Dates* & Figs, Peaches, Passion Fruit*, Plums, Pears*, Kiwi, Nectarines‡, Grapes*†, Cherries*, Cantaloupe, Currants*, Raisins*, Tangerines‡, and Tomatoes (in season).

*High Iron
†Cleansers (must be organic)
‡As juice must be combined with just a tad of lemon for orange and lime for grapefruit.

- **Fats**
  - Cashews, Almonds*, Natural Peanut Butter, Almond Butter, Raw Cheese, Walnuts, Pecans, Filberts, Coconut, Peanuts, and Pine Nuts.

*High Iron (4.4 mg), High Calcium (245 mg), and High Phosphorus (475 mg).

- **Healthy Mixed-Snacks**

Mixed Nuts
Pure Bars

Active Green Bars

VEGAN

- ❖ Consume a well-balanced vegetable diet, including principally those things that will provide iron.
- ❖ Fat and protein at every meal. Consume enough healthy fats, as a vegan diet is naturally low in fat:
    - o Flaxseed oil, coconut oil, or raw milk, almond butter, cashew butter, peanut butter, etc. are all excellent sources.
    - o

Remember, although body weight is a function of the balance between ***energy*** intake and ***energy*** expenditure, at times increases or decreases in food intake fail to produce the expected change in body weight. This is because the body can sometimes make adjustments in ***energy*** expenditure to coincide with changes in ***energy*** intake. The brain uses this information to coordinate adjustments in ***energy*** intake and expenditure to maintain ***energy*** balance on both a long—and a short-term basis.

ENERGY SYSTEM TRAINING

Know that your ***energy*** system training has an indirect effect on increasing the amount of calories you expend daily. Accordingly, the type of "cardio" you perform helps to create a caloric deficit and will assist in your fat loss. Basically, your cardio serves to increasingly activate your stored fat for usage in producing the ***energy*** desired for your training as well as your ***energy*** expenditure during immediate post training recovery. Aerobic training causes the heart to increase in size and strength, and it causes an increase in the amount of blood in your physique. These two adaptations to aerobic training are highly beneficial.

Preferably your ***energy*** system training intensity needs to range from 65% to 70%, or from 75% to 90% of your maximal heart rate. The Rhythmic Training Dance employs both for optimum training compliancy. Below this range you will have to perform the activity for a dreadfully long period of time.

- You can estimate your maximal heart rate by subtracting your age from 220, with a variation around this estimate of ±10 to 12 beats/min. For example, the estimated maximal heart rate for a 55-year old individual is: 220-55 (age in years) = 165 beats/min.

Thus the actual maximal heart rate for this person could be expected to fall within the range of 153 to 177 beats/min.

Our Rhythmic Training guides us to a space so deep and astounding that we want to dance, or to cry, or both at once, and which can almost madden us if we soar too long; however, going the distance reveals a splendor and beauty much like sleeping while facing the stars.

Our belief in the ***energy*** within us to achieve the physique we seek is a powerful moderator of our success with the Training Dance. It is very important to *educate, activate, and participate* to reap the incalculable benefits of living rhythmically with training and meditation. Having done this, developing realistic expectations and vigilance pays handsomely in living fear-free, claiming the ***energy*** of our power and with it our responsibility. The Mother/Father Source conducts the instrument of body and mind as the creative conduit through which the music of divinity flows: our voices, our hands, our hearts, and our very breath. ***Energy!***

You will be astounded at what happens when you repeatedly, forcefully, and positively follow the Rhythmic Dance of training to reach your short-term and long-term milestones. Once you can feel your power, that power can and will activate your inner resources toward attaining physique harmony and beauty.

No shame, train. No blame, train. Start where you are and train through to your milestones, rewards, and goals.

CHAPTER SEVEN: ELIXIRS OF LIFE

FIRST STEPS TOWARD OPTIMAL HEALTH

If we gain sufficient resistance to the seductions of chemistry, we will easily be led by the hand of Nature and soon recover our health and true happiness.
—Dr. John Lust

CLEANSING

In view of the fact that most people are toxic to a greater or lesser degree, a good quality cleansing regimen is the first step toward optimal health for anyone.

- First, see your physician for all medical conditions to obtain physician's clearance. If there are no abnormalities, you are ready to begin your expedition. The Rhythmic Training Dance will deliver the inspiration and the information. You must supply the acceptance and the perseverance.
- It is imperative to have a reliable scale on which you can weigh yourself the first thing every morning each Lunar Cycle: New Moon, First Quarter, Full Moon, and Last Quarter.

Begin a 3-day Apple Cleanse diet and have a colonic administered by a professional on day one.

Note that in no way is this a fast. You will be feeding your body through your blood with the necessary nutrients. A cleansing diet prevents the shrinking of your digestive organs, and also prevents lines and wrinkles in your face and physique.

Most importantly, the apples must be chemical-free "organic" Golden Yellow or Fuji because your purpose for this regimen is to cleanse your internal system.

DAY ONE

Consume as many unpeeled apples as you want. If for any reason you find apples distasteful, you can mix them in your blender into uncooked applesauce. Again, you must have a colonic sometime this day, or else your body will begin to reabsorb the toxins you are releasing from your lower colon. Take a brisk walk and some general stretching. Take a steam bath. Before retiring, take one tablespoon of 100 percent pure light olive oil (mix with hot water if you dislike oil).

DAY TWO

Consume as many apples as you desire, but if possible consume less than yesterday as this is a process of elimination as well as a semi-holiday for your digestive system. Have a colonic and a massage. Repeat olive oil in the evening.

DAY THREE

Continue apple consumption, but if possible, consume less than Day Two. Have another colonic and steam room. Conclude with the olive oil.

If you have no colonic hygienist services offered in your location, and neither access to a steam room nor dry sauna facility, see below.

STEAM

You may acquire a Combination Personal Hygiene and

Enema Water Bottle (Hot/Cold applications), a bottle of Food Grade Hydrogen Peroxide (H_2O_2), Organic Witch Hazel tincture, Calendula Oil, Two Gallons Distilled Water, Liquid DMSO (70%DMSO/30%Distilled Water), a spray bottle, a measuring cup, a box of Epsom Salt, Baking Soda, and your favorite fragranced candle.

- Dilute H_2O_2 as directed and pour into spray bottle.
- Mist your entire body thoroughly and stand in a hot shower allowing the steam to engulf you for about 10 minutes.
- Draw a bath: Add 8 ounces of Food Grade Hydrogen Peroxide (H_2O_2) to a tub of warm water, slip in and relax for at least 20 minutes (candle light optional, yet favorable).
- Again, mist your entire body to restore the natural protective acid mantle of your skin. (Soap used while bathing/showering removes this protective acid mantle.)

ENEMA

- A possible three-phase enema method.
    - Organize all materials and a kettle of boiling spring water.

- First Phase: Ready the enema bag setup. Sterilize all parts, especially the hose and nozzle. One quart of water will be required as follows: From the kettle fill the cup, and add one teaspoon each of soda and salt. Dilute thoroughly by stirring. Pour into bag. Add three more cups of distilled water for a lukewarm solution.

- Apply calendula oil both to the nozzle and your rectum. Relax. Lie on your left side, and gradually dilate your rectum, inhale while working the nozzle into place.
- Manipulate the shut-off clamp to control the speed at which the water enters to avert cramping. When you feel you are unable to hold the water, close your eyes, take deep breaths and close the clamp until the intense sensation subsides.
- After you have taken in the quart of water, hold as long as possible before expelling.

- Second Phase: Repeat all the steps of the first phase (including sterilization). Relax. Assume a knee-chest position on all fours and take in your second quart of water. Upon expelling of your second quart, rest a moment.
- Final Phase: Take your third quart, in which you have added one teaspoon each of organic witch hazel, food grade H_2O_2, and liquid DMSO instead of the soda and salt. Take your last enema lying on your right side.
    - For a more thorough cleansing get up and walk around before you expel this last enema.
    -

Create a calming atmosphere by lighting your desired fragranced candle (optional, yet favorable).

DAILY CLEANSING ENEMA

- Acquire a Latex–free portable rectal syringe.
  - Continual physiological hygiene gives strength and vigor to your body and prolongs life.
  - Daily intestinal cleanliness includes internal washing of your colon and rectum which make for freedom from autointoxication and constipation.
  - Cleanse your tongue by scraping to remove the sediment that settles on it during sleep and, which, if ignored, decays. Cleanse your ears and nostrils as well.

This structure of hygiene may seem peculiar, yet it is even more important to keep the interior of your body clean than the surface of your skin. Most daily bowel movements are a partial evacuation, giving off only the end portion of a decaying fecal mass. By constant practice, intestinal cleanliness is essential for progress in mental, physical, and spiritual rejuvenation.

Prudent Weight Loss

Following your cleansing, you can begin a four days on, two days off grape (seedless varieties) diet. You may ingest as many grapes as you desire throughout the day and consume plenty of water—at least six eight ounce glasses per day. Water assists in dissolving the nutritive substances in the course of digestion, so that it is assimilated through your physique to repair and remove waste as well as temperature regulation.

❖ Water with fresh cut lemons is a great cleanser and refresher beverage for your physique.

This is followed by two days off.

A two-day menu sample:

❖ Lacto-vegetarian

CHEEZY BREAD

2 slices Ezekiel Bread

Organic Raw Sharp Cheese

2.5 ounces Henry & Lisa's Tuna

Distribute tuna over slices of bread, cover with slices of cheese, heat and serve.

JUICING

Begin juicing for five (5) days. Every 2.5 to 3 hours juice and ingest:

1 cup strawberries

1 cup blueberries

1 cup raspberries

2 scoops hemp protein powder (30g)

Be sure to ingest plenty of lemon water throughout the day.

❖ **Vegetarian**

15 ounces (425g) lentils

2 slices Ezekiel Bread

Repeat the five days juicing and two days off with sample menu.

FASTING

- If you choose to fast **or** abstain from all stimulants—coffee, tea, meat, fish, eggs, salt, pepper, mustard, tobacco, sugar, alcohol, and television—FOR ONE DAY, it can give your magnificent physique system a chance to purify itself of toxic substances.

- Know that fasting means no ingesting of anything for the entire day until the next day. Additionally, your purpose is defeated if you ingest too much food after your fast.
- Short-term fasts of one or two days are very constructive mentally, physically, and spiritually, particularly when sufficient hydration with water is maintained in correlation with focused deep breathing (preferably in the open air). Abundance of oxygen accelerates elimination and burns up toxins.

EACH MORNING

- As soon as your feet hit the ground, massage your toes on the ground as if you are trying to pick up a tiny ball.

BREATH

Oxygen is one of the best blood purifiers and one of the most effective nerve tonics, as it flows through your sympathetic and central nervous system, which are intimately related with your cardiorespiratory function. It is simply provided by nature for all. Functional training in the open air will bring new strength and vitality and give a happy and cheerful attitude of mind. Proper training in the open air and sunshine are among God's greatest gifts to us all. Life is more dependent upon the regular and adequate supply of oxygen than any other element. You may live for many days without solid food, and several days without even liquid food, but death comes swiftly without air.

By learning to regulate your breath, you are obtaining control of the cosmic electrical ***energy*** in the ambient air taken into your body. When cosmic rays strike the earth's atmosphere, they condense into electrified minerals, which are taken into your body with each breath and offer a superior form of mineral-vitamin nourishment.

Consequently, it is vital to integrate rhythmic, slow, and controlled breathing into your training practice. It leads to voluntary control over the basic physiological functioning of your physique. A physique without motion is heading toward rigor mortis, and to prevent this from occurring, it has to move. For instance, after six to eight hours of sleep, one feels invigorated and rested, yet after ten to twelve hours, one awakens feeling like a train or truck has hit them because of the inactivity of about fourteen or so hours. Thus, training has no Holidays or Shabbats! Even on your off days, stay in the open air as much as possible. You exercise by simply walking briskly. In the city, early morning walks are preferable. This brings better oxygen quality to your blood circulation.

BREATH PRACTICE

- First, imagine the electrical ***energy*** flow with each inhalation.
- Rise on your toes, simultaneously raising your arms out to the side and then up over your head, inhaling deeply through your nostrils.
- Exhale sharply through your mouth while bringing your arms down.
- Lower your heels, crossing your arms and hugging yourself at the waist as you bend

forward, releasing all the air from your lungs.

- Forcefully contract your abdominals to exhale any remaining air before beginning your next inhalation.
- Repeat for 3 minutes. As you progress in respiratory control, the duration of these being extended to 5 to 6 minutes gradually begin inhaling through alternate nostrils. As you breathe alternately, first through one nostril and then through the other (close your right nostril with your right thumb, raise your left arm; and when closing your left nostril with your left thumb, raise your right arm) with each inhalation. Your continued psychic imagining of these processes aids tremendously in their fulfillment.
- Always terminate the exercise by exhaling through your left nostril.

FINE MOTOR MAINTENANCE

EYES

In lieu of the current usage of visual technology, the training of your eyes is imperative because if your eyes are injured or strained, this affects the entire nervous system. Transmission of forces and limitations to movement can occur given that your nervous tissue is involved with all of the sensory, motor, and reflex activities of your muscles. All of your abilities to see, feel, touch, move, orient yourself, and interact with your environment are the result of the communication between nervous tissue and specialized tissues, such as skeletal muscle.

Starting Position:Sit erect (the chest held up and out with the chin pulled in and back) with *head remaining stationary throughout entire movement*. All exercises start in this position.

I

Action:

- Extend your left arm forward, holding index finger extended and raised upright.
- Gradually bend your elbow, moving arm and finger towards nose, following the motion with both eyes until they are virtually crossed as finger touches your nose.
- Extend your elbow to starting position following with eyes.

II

Action:

- Sit erect (the chest held up and out with the chin pulled in and back) with *head remaining stationary throughout entire movement*.
- Gently, with your palms facing up, lift your fully extended left arm out to the side aligning at shoulder height.
- Begin rotating your index finger.
- While moving your arm in a circular motion to the center of your head, simultaneously, engage both eyes by rolling them to the extreme left and following your finger motion up to the top of the socket, then extreme right and down to the bottom of the socket.

- Pause for a second in each position.
- Repeat with right hand, with eyes rolling in opposite direction.

III

Action:

- Firmly shut your eyes. Hold for a count of five.
- Rest for a count of five. Repeat.
- Slowly open wide. Hold for five seconds.
- Repeat twice.
- Close eyes. Hollow your palms and cover eyes (never touch your eyeballs).
- Rest eyes by imagining blackness.

HEAD, NECK, and FACE

Exclamation Surprise and Sour (face and neck)

Starting Position: Sit erect (the chest held up and out with the chin pulled in and back), hands on your lap, and eyes closed with head remaining stationary throughout entire movement.

Action:

- Try to make your eyes, nose, chin, and cheeks squeeze to a point in the center of your face. Pucker your lips, flatten your chin, and wrinkle the bridge of your nose.
- Squeeze. Pause. Then repeat.

Obicularis Oculi (face)

Lower Lid Local

Starting Position: Sit erect (the chest held up and out with the chin pulled in and back, hands on your lap. Look straight ahead, eyes open.

Action:

- Gently and slowly move your lower eyelids up and down. Concentrate and practice. Try not to involve your cheeks and eyebrows. Do not close your eyes as in squinting, but try to close your eyes with the lower lids.
- Repeat.

Forehead Glide (face and neck)

Starting Position:Sit erect (the chest held up and out with the chin pulled in and back), eyes closed. Place your index fingers directly under your eyebrows, fingertips resting comfortably at the roof of your nose.

Action:

- Press the forehead down with fingertips remaining in place. Keep your neck aligned with your spine, making the muscles of your forehead do the work.
- Repeat.

Orbicularis Oris (face and neck)

Starting Position:Sit erect (the chest held up and out with the chin pulled in and back), hands on your lap, with eyes open.

Action:

- Pull the corners of your mouth down as your chin points upward.
- Relax.
- Try the left corner, then the right. Then repeat.

RELAXATION

Starting Position:Sit aligned with feet flat on the floor

(no socks), eyes closed.

I

Action:

- Spread your toes. Imagine each toe touching the floor from your little toes to your big toes, and out again. Then spread your toes as the front of your foot presses downward, gently raising your heels.
- Slowly lower.
- Repeat. Then relax.

II

Starting Position:Sit comfortably with your spine aligned, hands on your lap.

Action:

- Take a deep breath. When you're ready to exhale, pull your diaphragm in suddenly, exhaling through your nose quickly.
- Relax. Then repeat slowly.
- Concentrate on breathing as deeply as you comfortably can.

SLEEP

Stress can be greatly diminished and its perverse affects alleviated by carefully planned training to include holistic meals and adequate sleep. Training assists in adjusting sleep habits. Remember, health and sweet sleep will come to you when you need, unless by deleterious habits you drive them away.

- Close your eyes and place your head and neck in a comfortable position.
- Inhale fully as much as possible through your

nostrils.

- Fully focus upon your breathing, imagining the breath passing from your nostrils.
- Bring your mind to conceive this, blocking out all other thoughts and ideas.
- Keep your eyes closed and all your consciousness and memory will gradually be dispelled.

Sleep!

PRAYER HELPS YOU PLAN, PREPARE AND GROW

Prayers are excellent for strengthening and harmonizing your focus and concentration. Prayer denotes honesty, responsibility, and humility through the valleys of realignment and living well.

The Specificity Prayer reaffirms and gives voice and clarity to your intentions and puts the Universe on notice, "I AM ready." Use it to release everything you think you know about spirituality, healthy dieting, and changing negative living patterns that you may begin and continue to have an open heart and an open mind to celebrate, support, and nurture productive positivity with all these things.

Practice this prayer throughout your transformation process as the waves of your fears, insecurities, and vulnerability emerge and submerge throughout your process.

Specificity Prayer

Beloved Spirit Force,

Sometimes I think that I want to let go of fearful unhealthy living, yet I change nothing. I hold on to the fear and ingest the same nutrition deficient diet over and over, and in my mind thinking that soon I will feel and look better.

Still I know that this is never the answer to making things better or to making me feel better. Living, thinking, and dieting this way only perpetuates the problem, for each time I stop and begin again, the fear and weight return with friends and my heart becomes heavier.

I AM ready to admit I have no clue. I know that changing is necessary for my own well-being. If I hold on to this way of living, thinking, and dieting, I AM opening the door to adverse health and undesired outcomes.

I want to follow the Training Dance Shades.

Help me relax, release, know and let go.

Help me know that only I can take these actions. I *must* act.

Help me have the courage to release the old ways of living, thinking, dieting, and feelings of fatigue, and see myself through the eyes of divine love.

Thank You.

CHAPTER EIGHT: EXPRESSIONS OF STRENGTH

LET'S DANCE THE ART OF CHOOSING

> Absorb what is useful. Reject what is useless, and add what is specifically your own.
> –Bruce Lee

Our bodies are stunningly majestic **energy** systems capable of moving in almost every imaginable direction, and our muscles provide the impetus for movement. Our joint arrangements transmit this power into the gross pushing, pulling, and rotating forces that our bodies are able to create.

<u>It is a statistical fact that muscle fitness</u> can improve through the ninth decade of life and is correlated with maintaining and improving health cognitively, physically, psychologically, as well as fiscally. Without strength, our muscles can generate minimal force. You may have heard people describe certain exercises as strength exercises or power exercises. However, this has no validity. Power is the mathematical product of force and velocity at the speed of your exercise. And power is intimately tied to work. Our focus for work is your body's ability to function and move pain-free with relative ease and grace. Therefore, strength and power are what separate less mobile persons from vibrantly active persons.

When our muscles are weak and we attempt to

perform activities, the body will recruit whatever muscles it can to perform these movements. Essentially, the body begins asking certain muscles to perform a function that they are not intended to do. As a result of this, the muscles are working in force ranges that are beyond their capabilities. The connection point—the joints—typically suffers some sort of injury as a result.

Researchers have noted that, standing weight exercises are the best form of anti-gravitational resistance training available—better than machines, better than cables. The reason for this is because when we are standing and supporting free weight, every muscle in the body must be contracting. Machines are unable to recruit stabilizer muscles. Therefore, machines are unable to mimic real world scenarios.

The reason the isolated body part training on machines do not work is the same reason that barbells (BB) work so well, better than any other implements we can use to gain strength. The human physique functions as a complete system—it works that way, and it favors being trained that way. Consequently, since barbells, and the primary exercises we use them to do, are far superior to any other training implements that have ever been devised, a mind-muscle connection must be instilled for living health for the long term.

Properly performed, full range-of-motion barbell exercises are essentially the functional expression of human skeletal and muscular anatomy under a load. The exercise is controlled by and the result of each individual's particular movement patterns, minutely fine-tuned by each individual limb length, muscular attachment position, strength level, flexibility, and neuromuscular efficiency. Balance between all the muscles involved in a movement is inherent in the training, since all the muscles involved contribute their anatomically-determined share of the work. Muscles move the joints between the bones which transfer force to the load, and the way this is done is a function of the design of the system—when that system is employed in a manner of its design, it functions *optimally,* and training must follow this design. Barbells allow weight to be moved exactly the way your body is designed to move it, since every aspect of the movement is determined by your body.

Structural Exercises: What and How

Sufficient evidence exists that the squat is most effective for increasing your bone mineral density (BMD). Therefore, structural exercises are best: the back squat, power clean, deadlift, snatch, and push press (axial skeleton and lower body) and the shoulder press (for the upper body) to increase your bone strength. Every major muscle group is accounted for with these exercises.

The majority of time performing resistance training movements will be spent performing the following:

- Knee dominant exercises (different kinds of squats)
- Hip dominant exercises (deadlift variations & bridge variations)
- Upper body vertical pushing (military press variations)
- Upper body vertical pulling (pull-up variations)
- Upper body horizontal pushing (bench press

variations)

- Upper body horizontal pulling (rowing variations)
- and torso/abdominals (anti-extension & anti-rotation)

The most basic, multijoint exercise for developing your lower body is the squat. The primary muscles used during these exercises are your quadriceps and your hip extensors (glutei and hamstrings). However, overall, squatting engages the greater articulation of your ankles, knees, and hips. There are limitless sub-types of the 2 foot squat. That being said, there are some commonalities between all versions of the 2 footed squat.

❖ Here is an annotated list:

1. Feet are generally flat on the floor.
2. Weight is on your heels.
3. You try to "spread the floor" with your feet.
4. Your lumbar spine is held in an arch.
5. Your glutei are shifted downward and backward.
6. Your chest is held high with thoracic spine extension.
7. Your knees are pushed laterally.
8. The barbell remains directly over the middle of the foot.
9. On the ascent, your glutei are contracted maximally.
10. On the ascent, the top of your head is driven towards the ceiling.
11. Your eyes look straight ahead.

There are 2 kinds of 2 footed barbell squats—the front squat & the back squat. The front squat involves squatting while the barbell rests on the anterior shoulders. The back squat involves squatting while the barbell rests on the posterior shoulders and trapezius muscles.

<u>Front Squat</u>

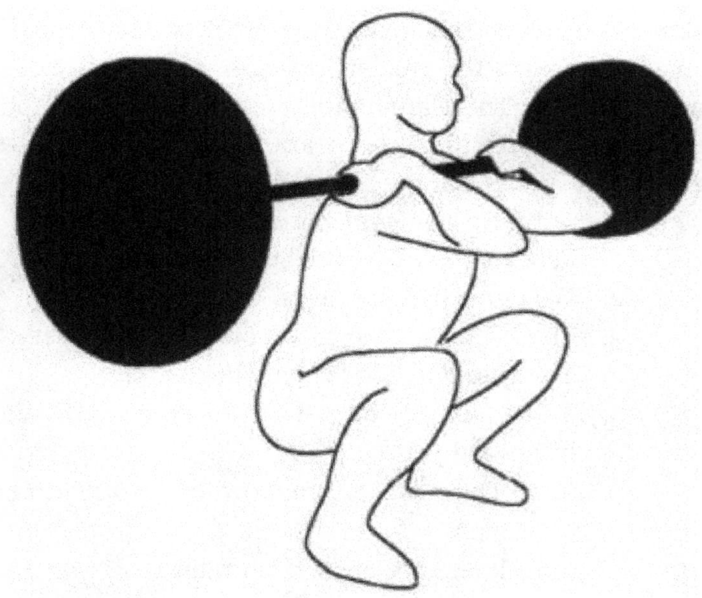

Technique of the Front Squat

- ❖ The front squat is characterized as a 2 footed squat where the barbell is placed on your anterior shoulders.
  - o Your fingers are under the barbell, but the barbell rests on your shoulders.
  - o Your elbows are pointed as high as possible

and are directed medially.

- On your descent, focus on spreading the floor with your feet, moving your knees laterally, maintaining a tight lumbar spine arch, maintaining thoracic spine extension, holding your elbows up and in, lowering your hips to a position below the knees with your glute muscles, and sitting between your calves.
- On the ascent, push the floor away from yourself using your knee extensors, continue to push your knees laterally, contract your glutei muscles maximally, drive your elbows up towards the ceiling, and accelerate through the end of the movement.

Olympic Style Squat

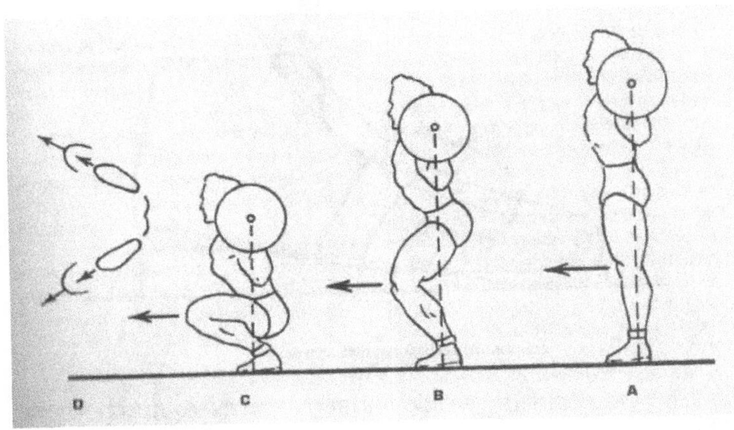

Technique of the Olympic Style Squat

The Olympic style back squat features a 2 foot squat where your torso is held more vertically in comparison to the powerlifting style back squat.

- ❖ In the Olympic style back squat, you hold the bar in what is called the, "high carry position."
  - o The bar is higher up towards the neck.
- ❖ In the Olympic style back squat, your knees move anterior to your toes.
- ❖ The Olympic style back squat is a much more knee dominant squatting style compared to the more hip dominant powerlifting style back squat.
- ❖ Proper Olympic style back squatting requires exceptional ankle mobility to perform.

<u>Powerlifting Back Squat</u>

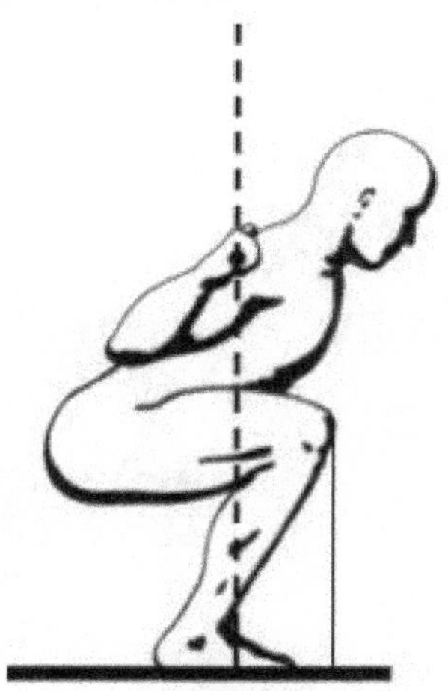

The powerlifting back squat features a much more acute torso angle compared to the Olympic style back squat.

- ❖ The Olympic style back squat and the front squat are more truly knee dominant exercises.
- ❖ The powerlifting style back squat is more of a

hybrid knee/hip movement with no dominance placed on either joint.

Both styles feature the weight on your heels, with your feet "spreading the floor," your knees moving laterally, your lower back arched, and your thoracic spine being held in extension, as well as the other entire commonalities shared by all squat styles.

The Deadlift

Variations of the 2 footed Deadlift

There are 2 classic variations of the standard deadlift

1. The Romanian deadlift:
   - The individual keeps the lumbar spine

in a tight arch and the thoracic spine extended.
   - The individual keeps the knees slightly flexed.
   - The individual pushes the hips back until the bar is at the level of the knees, then pushes the hips forward to return to standing.
2. The stiff-legged deadlift:
   - Same as the Romanian deadlift; however, our knees are kept fully extended.
   - Never go lower than where you can keep a tight lower back arch and an extended thoracic spine.

Remember your primary movement with deadlifting is hip extension.

<u>Bridging</u>

The Bridge is our Other Hip Dominant Exercise

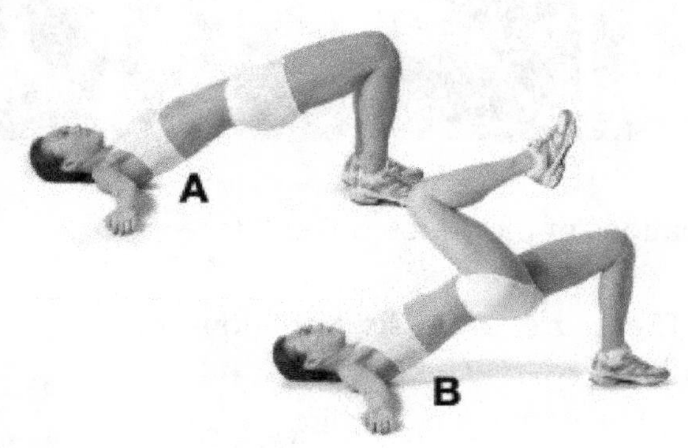

- The primary purpose for bridging is to work on hip extension, particularly contracting your glutei muscles.
- Based on EMG analysis, nothing causes greater levels of glutei activation than bridging exercises.
    - There are a number of different bridge variations; however, the two most common are the 2 footed and the single footed versions

<u>Spinal Flexion (Kyphotic Back): Absolute Disaster</u>

The primary way that people hurt themselves during 2 foot barbell lifts is by moving their lumbar and thoracic spine into a flexed (kyphotic) position

- ❖ The cardinal rule to follow in any weight training session *is to never let the back roll over.*

Horizontal Pushing – The Bench Press

The bench press and its variants are the primary exercises to strengthen your horizontal pushing movement pattern. The variations include the dumbbell (DB) bench press.

The bench press requires you having 5 points of contact:

- o Both feet must be touching the ground
- o Your glutei must touch the bench
- o Both shoulder blades must be in contact with the bench
- o Your head must be in contact with the bench

Technique of the Bench Press

- Ideal technique for your bench press involves the following:
    - Trying to keep your feet flat on the ground.
    - Trying to move your feet as close to being under your hips as possible.
    - A tight arch in your lower back.
    - Your scapula retracted as forcefully as possible.
    - Your abdominals contracted as forcefully as possible.
    - Gripping the bar as hard as possible.
    - Try to "pull the bar apart" laterally with your hands.
    - Lower the bar to the xiphoid process of the sternum.
    - To raise the bar, try to push yourself away from the. Bar
    - Your bar-path on the way up should be either directly vertical, or pressed in the direction back towards the rack of the bench.

<u>Spinal/Torso/Abdominals</u>

"Core" is an exercise "buzz word" that has been used to mystify you and make you believe that there are secret exercises that work secret body parts. But originally, the term "core exercises" referred to 2 foot, 2 hand barbell exercises that were considered to be the "core" exercises of any legitimate strength training regimen. Presently, the word core gets tossed about with people doing all sorts of ridiculous exercises on ridiculous pieces of equipment.

Where is this "core"? Have we suddenly become apples? Are there seeds in the center of our bodies, or maybe there's a pit? Let's call it what it is. We have abdominal wall muscles that attach to our rib cage, sternum, and inominate (hip) bone. We have spinal erectors and spinal rotators that attach to our vertebrae and our rib cage. We have glutes and hip flexors that attach to the lower aspects of our vertebrae (lumbar, sacrum, coccyx), and our femur. There are better words to describe these exercises than "core" - real anatomical names, or at the very least practical names that everyone can understand.

These exercises are more accurately deemed torso exercises, and some are more specifically hip exercises. Everybody knows what their torso is and everybody knows what their hips are. Let's all start using words that make sense. If an exercise effectively trains the muscles of your torso or your hips then it has many benefits. I've seen and heard a lot of talking about "core" exercises, and when I see what they are doing, I want to regurgitate.

- Your torso and hip area that we are interested in training includes the following:
  - Your diaphragm is the upper boundary.
  - Your hip girdle is the lower boundary.
  - Abdominal muscles in front.
  - Paraspinals and glutei in back.
  - This region contains 29 pairs of muscles that hold your trunk steady, and balance and stabilize the bony structures of your spine, pelvis, thorax, and other kinetic chain structures activated during most movements.
  - When these spine-frame structures do not have adequate strength and stability, we become mechanically unstable.

Properly Functioning Torso & Hip Muscles

When your 29 muscles in question are functioning properly, your body is able to transfer forces appropriately from your lower segments (legs) to your upper segments (arms) and vice versa. Optimal control and efficiency of movements are improved; adequate absorption of ground impact forces can be accomplished with a decrease in ***energy*** lost as heat during movement is seen.

Succinctly the correct exercises for your torso training are Anti-extension exercises and Anti-rotation exercises.

- ❖ Anti-extension exercises
  - – The plank is the basic anti-extension exercise.
  - – Progressions to advanced stages of the plank include:
    - o The abdominal wheel roll-outs, the stacking plank, foot elevated plank, push up rows, etc.
- ❖ Anti-rotation exercises
  - – Anti-rotation presses are the primary anti-rotation exercise.
    - o Also, landmine exercises strengthen this function.

Please freely peruse the current library of exercises and videos. There is no way that we could ever cover and describe all of these exercises in this chapter.

Nothing gives more "bang for your buck" than weightlifting exercises. They can lead to ***all*** of the positive strength training adaptations that are considered to be most important from a physiological standpoint. That being said, they are not the end-all, be-all of strength and training. They are another implement to be used within a quality, well-rounded health regimen. It just so happens that they are perhaps the most indispensible and valuable implement available today. The other take away point is that "more is not always better" with weightlifting exercises–quality reigns the day as previously mentioned.

Remember that everyone has these fundamental movement patterns during normal growth and development. However, people lose these patterns when they focus on one aspect of movement or performance.

Our modern lifestyles and our societal concepts of "proper fitness techniques" have caused us to lose the movement qualities that our species is supposed to be able to demonstrate.

The Disclaimer

The strength training theory and exercises that are being presented are intended to be used by individuals who possess the underlying functional movement capabilities that are considered to be pre-requisites to such a training regimen. If you utilize the methods presented prior to having a functional movement base, you are in essence, "putting the cart before the horse," "building a house of cards," "building a castle in the sand," or whatever other cliché saying you want to insert. Therefore, be wise, be prudent, and precise.

Transform Your Life! A Sample 28 Week Program

When we boil everything down, the whole point of spiritual and strength training is to cause adaptations within our mind, our nervous system, and our skeletal muscle system, so **let's dance and evolve our full** range expression of strength!

MEDITATIVE AFFIRMATIONS

By stating your daily affirmations aloud, they will be even more powerful because your affirmation will involve three physical components: vision, speech, and hearing. Your affirmations shall have the strength and support of your mind, body, and soul. All the muscles and motor learning functions that are engaged in your visual, verbal, and auditory processes will be set in motion guiding you toward your Rhythmic Training day. Thus, the more power the affirmations shall have and the more foundation and focus you will have for the day's activities. Employ your strong, solid, supportive voice!

FOUNDATION SHADE

Begin to use the ***energy*** in color as an interactive reinforcement. There are no firm rules as to what must be said or done. Just understand that color is like a "key" unlocking a distinct chamber of your involuntary mind. And the basic simple fact that each color carries its vibratory effects, releasing ***energy*** at a certain rate of speed and that frequency, or "wave length," ***energizes*** a distinct part of your being as it penetrates your aura. These powerful impulses are transmitted to your brain along the nervous routes just like your impulses for movement.

Simply keep an open mind and a willing attitude. Relax, release, and let go of your controversial conditioning and all that you have been taught so you can simply know and have fun transforming your spirit and physique.

Black and White are symbolic of joy and balance, respectively. Throughout this Shade, simply pay attention to where and how black and white appear in the world as you practice surrendering to a new physique balance of health and joy. Decide what you are going to eat. Meal preparation is indispensable. Keep in mind a balance of nutrition—the relationship of foods to your optimal health.

WEEK ONE

Sunday

Attitude

- You must fully embrace and love your body exactly as it is today. This exercise in support can be profitably practiced daily.
- This enables you to be human and imperfectly perfect now. Being resolved, this practice during training can be the foundation upon which increased mental health and therefore spiritual and physical progress can be strengthened.

Affirmation: I AM aware that my old way of dieting was a very unnatural way of feeding. Thus, I will say thank you to the Spirit Force for everything. My whole attitude toward living healthy will be one of gratitude. I anticipate that more truths will flow in my new way of being alive.

DAY ONE

Exercise	Sets	Reps	Percentage	Rest	Comments
Warm-up and Stretching					
Bench Press	3	10	67%1RM	90 seconds	
Lateral Raise	3	10	55%RM	60 seconds	
Triceps Extension	3	10	"	60 seconds	
Abdominals Bent-knee Sit-up	3	12		45 seconds	
***Cardio: 19 minutes**			Warm-up 5 minutes then Fast as possible @ Level 6-10 for 1 minute Recovery pace @ Level 3-5 for 2 minutes **Repeat 3 Times** Then Cool down 5 minutes		

*Sessions will consist of bike, stepper, elliptical, rowing, swimming, walking, stationary bike, treadmill, or any other cardiovascular activity.

Monday

Words and Actions

- It is an absolute necessity that you begin to rhythmically train, but be objective with no aim of arriving there quickly—there is no there.
- Remember that the first and by far the most essential ingredient necessary to reaching your spiritual and physical goal is begin to train. Period!

Affirmation: I AM keeping an open mind and following this dance one session at a time. I ask to use each training moment well.

DAY TWO

Exercise	Sets	Reps	Percentage	Rest	Comments
Warm-up and Stretching					
Back Squat	3	10	67%1RM	90 seconds	
Lunges	3	10	"	90 seconds	
Abdominals: Crunch **Cardio:** Brisk Walk **20 minutes**	3	15		35 seconds	

Tuesday
Discipline in Ownership

- Training your mind, body, and soul is a way of life—a way of life you can learn through living the Training Dance Shades.
- The principles in this manual are like guide posts. They point the direction in which you have to go. But you must remember: You have to find your own best way to live the training dance way of life. This book will help you learn to train regularly, that it becomes a natural way of living.

Affirmation: I will relax, release, and control my breathing. I AM learning the benefits of poised-strength and spirit-balance in developing the physique I seek. I pray that I may subject myself to this discipline of strength and be free from all angst. I pray that I may begin each session relaxed.

DAY THREE

Exercise	Sets	Reps	Percentage	Rest	Comments
Warm-up and Stretching					
LatPulldown	3	10	67%RM	90 seconds	
Seated Row	3	10	"	90 seconds	
Bicep Curl	3	10	55%RM	60 seconds	
Abdominals: Bent-knee	3	12		35	

Sit-up ***Cardio: 19 minutes**			Warm-up 5 minutes then Fast as possible @ Level 6-10 for 1 minute Recovery pace @ Level 3-5 for 2 minutes **Repeat 3 Times** Then Cool down	seconds	

*Sessions will consist of bike, stepper, elliptical, rowing, swimming, walking, stationary bike, treadmill, or any other cardiovascular activity.

Wednesday

Lessons of Torment

- ➢ What dreadful spiritual and physical punishment incomplete dieting and stress puts on your body systems—the arterial plaque and inefficient circulation, the agitated digestion and sluggish elimination.
- ➢ When you begin to holistically diet and navigate the Training Dance, your body systems

begin to experience functional freedoms. True escape from punishment necessitates your continued willingness to adhere to, and apply, the key of rhythmic training actions as needed to turn the lock. With the appropriate application of action, both the lock and the bars of spiritual and physical punishment will open for you.

Affirmation: I AM walking the way of healthier living; it may mean a complete reversal of the way of dieting and thinking which I previously practiced. But it is a reversal that leads to stress-free living and happiness. I desire to cease being overly-indulgent in fears, foods and practices that cause cruelty and punishment to my physical, mental, and spiritual health.

DAY FOUR

Exercise	Sets	Reps	Percentage	Rest	Comments
Warm-up and Stretching					
Abdominals: Ab Wheel	3	10		40 seconds	
***Cardio: 20-25 minutes**			Steady-State @ 70 – 75% predicted maximum heart rate		

*Sessions will consist of bike, stepper, elliptical,

rowing, swimming, walking, stationary bike, treadmill, or any other cardiovascular activity.

Thursday

Perseverance

- Beginning training can be like the wilderness plains. The Training Dance is more a way of building a new life than just a way to lose fear and weight. You have "gone on a diet" plenty of times. And of course, you always started and went off your diet because you were only waiting for the time when you could "get-off a diet." This cycle only makes the weight worse and worse.

Affirmation: I AM getting better and better. It is in the daily sessions that perseverance counts. I know that no effort is too small. I ask that I will continue doing what is best. I pray to persevere and so find physique health, harmony, and beauty.

DAY FIVE

Exercise	Sets	Reps	Percentage	Rest	Comments
Warm-up and Stretching					
Bench Press	3	10	67%1RM	90 seconds	
Lateral Raise	3	10	55%RM	60 seconds	
Triceps Extension	3	10	"	60 seconds	

Abdominals: Bent-knee Sit-up	3	12		45 seconds	
***Cardio: 19 minutes**			Warm-up 5 minutes then Fast as possible @ Level 6-10 for 1 minute Recovery pace @ Level 3-5 for 2 minutes **Repeat 3 Times** Then Cool down 5 minutes		

*Sessions will consist of bike, stepper, elliptical, rowing, swimming, walking, stationary bike, treadmill, or any other cardiovascular activity.

Friday

An Anchor

➢ You are engaged in training and holistic feedings. This is a pre-requisite to sensibly maintaining your health. Rhythmic Training means devotion to leading your body to do what it was designed to do—move gracefully. Your mobility and joint health will only be limited by your mental, physical, and spiritual development.

Affirmation: I AM being firm, balanced, beautiful, and focused daily. I aspire to use the art of ***energy*** balancing to redefine my body.

DAY SIX

Exercise	Sets	Reps	Percentage	Rest	Comments
Warm-up and Stretching					
Back Squat	3	10	67%1RM	90 seconds	
Lunges	3	10	"	90 seconds	
Abdominals: Crunch	3	15		35 seconds	
Cardio: Brisk Walk **20 minutes**					

Saturday OFF

Secret Storms

- Am I emotionally dependent on food? Am I using food to fight sexual frustration? Fear? Anger?

- You are learning to rhythmically train so as to act, and so diet each day that you are naturally, at all times, at peace with being yourself. Training is positive building, positive thinking, and positively seeking the cause and effect of Spirit throughout your life.

Affirmation: I AM loving my body in both the quiet and the din. I AM ingesting more naturally my size, my shape, and my texture, as well as my flavor. I pray to see myself fresh and new, as after a storm all looks washed, clean, and bright. I pray that such insight, vision, and understanding shall be mine.

DAY SEVEN

REST	**COMMENTS**
Abdominals	

WEEK TWO

Sunday

Surrender

- I know that Spirit Force cares for me. Thus, I surrender. I let go of my feelings of fearful resistance and open myself up to resistance training.

Affirmation: I center myself in the Spirit Force. I AM

doing this non-submissively, but enthusiastically and eagerly. I pray to follow the guidance that leads to the very best for me. I pray to walk this path of wholeness, health, joy, and stress free living.

DAY ONE

Exercise	Sets	Reps	Percentage	Rest	Comments
Warm-up and Stretching					
Bench Press	3	10	70%1RM	90 seconds	
Lateral Raise	3	10	55%1RM	60 seconds	
Triceps Extension	3	10	"	60 seconds	
Abdominals: Bent-knee Sit-up	3	12		45 seconds	
***Cardio: 19 minutes**			Warm-up 5 minutes then Fast as possible @ Level 6-10 for 1 minute Recovery pace @		

			Level 3-5 for 2 minutes **Repeat 3 Times** Then Cool down 5 minutes		

*Sessions will consist of bike, stepper, elliptical, rowing, swimming, walking, stationary bike, treadmill, or any other cardiovascular activity.

Monday
Honesty

- Suppressing yourself and your true feelings with food and fear are a form of self-deprecation, and the pressure of your suppression and pain only hurts you and everyone around you.
- The Training Dance is a gradual discovery, recovery, rejuvenation, and return process resulting in a new self-image, life affirming attitude, spirit, and physique.

Affirmation: I AM facilitating my sexiness with my consumption and assimilation of ***energy*** powered meals. I pray to cease working against myself.

DAY TWO

Exercise	Sets	Reps	Percentage	Rest	Comments
Warm-up and Stretching					
Back Squat	3	10	70%1RM	90 seco nds	

Lunges	3	10	"	90 seconds	
Abdominals: Crunch	3	15		30 seconds	
Cardio: Brisk Walk **20 minutes**					

Tuesday

Action

- Am I running myself into debt–physically, emotionally, and spiritually?
- Today I will listen more carefully in silence. Perchance, I need to reevaluate my expectations, my behaviors, and my beliefs.
- I will be more receptive to the guidance I receive. This will help me to be more flexible, more ready and willing to continue my training.

Affirmation: I AM open to changing even if I think I know it all. Blessings are always evident. If for some reason I AM unable to see the evidence, I continue the Training Dance. I hold to my faith, flexibility, and holistic dieting as my rhythmic training actions. I pray to feel and listen more to the enduring rhythm of my own body.

DAY THREE

Exercise	Sets	Reps	Percentage	Rest	Comments
Warm-up and Stretching					
LatPulldown	3	10	70%1RM	90 seconds	
Seated Row	3	10	"	90 seconds	
Bicep Curl	3	10	55%1RM	60 seconds	
Abdominals: Bent-knee Sit-up	3	15		35 seconds	
***Cardio: 19 minutes**			Warm-up 5 minutes then Fast as possible @ Level 6-10 for 1 minute Recovery pace @ Level 3-5 for 2 minutes **Repeat 3 Times** Then Cool down		

*Sessions will consist of bike, stepper, elliptical, rowing, swimming, walking, stationary bike, treadmill,l or any other cardiovascular activity.

Wednesday
Integrity

- When you are fear-filled, nutrient-deficient, and overweight your joints carry an awful load. Each extra pound is four extra pounds on your joints.
- In being fear-filled and overweight, you are twice as large, and you are only half alive because of the pain and discomfort your joints and connective tissues harbor within. Consider the hours you can spend stronger and lighter in body posture and spirit.

Affirmation: I AM integrating and building up instead of inhibiting and tearing down my structural health. I AM resolving to improve my spiritual and joint ***integrity*** by training. I ask to be encouraged by the fact that my weakness can become my greatest asset.

DAY FOUR

Exercise	Sets	Reps	Percentage	Rest	Comments
Warm-up and Stretching					
Abdominals: Ab Wheel	3	15		40 seconds	
***Cardio: 20-25 minutes**			Steady-State @ 70 – 75%		

			predicted maximum heart rate		

*Sessions will consist of bike, stepper, elliptical, rowing, swimming, walking, stationary bike, treadmill, or any other cardiovascular activity.

Thursday

Progress

- When you look at most processed food packages, you see color enhanced decorations. But when you carefully read the labels of what is inside those packages, you see toxins. Poets tell us that "color is a spirit upon things by which they become expressive to the spirit." How are these chemicals and colors affecting your physical light and nerve processes?
- All the money in the world can never bring back first-class health.

Affirmation: I AM investing now in my short-term and long-term health through holistic dieting and training. I choose to make real progress toward a healthier life.

DAY FIVE

Exercise	Sets	Reps	Percentage	Rest	Comments
Warm-up and Stretching					
Bench Press	3	10	67%1RM	90 seconds	
Lateral Raise	3	10	55%RM	60 seconds	
Triceps					

Extension	3	10	"	60 seconds	
Abdominals: Bent-knee Sit-up	3	12		45 seconds	
***Cardio: 19 minutes**			Warm-up 5 minutes then Fast as possible @ Level 6-10 for 1 minute Recovery pace @ Level 3-5 for 2 minutes **Repeat 3 Times** Then Cool down 5 minutes		

*Sessions will consist of bike, stepper, elliptical, rowing, swimming, walking, stationary bike, treadmill, or any other cardiovascular activity.

Friday

Tolerance

- You are overcoming your initial aversion to holistic dieting and training, an aversion that upon evaporating presents you with mental, physical, and spiritual rejuvenation as it courses ***energy*** and fresh blood through your body systems.

Affirmation: I AM changing, training, and learning to accept, expect, and tolerate intervals of discomfort. I pray to accept the truth that my investment in training to sustain my health is much more pleasant than the investment of laboring to repair the ravages of ailments to regain my health.

DAY SIX

Exercise	Sets	Reps	Percentage	Rest	Comments
Warm-up and Stretching					
Back Squat	3	10	70%1RM	90 seconds	
Lunges	3	10	"	90 seconds	
Abdominals: Crunch	3	20		30 seconds	
Cardio: Brisk Walk **20 minutes**					

Saturday OFF
Humility

- You can hold fast to the truth that a body full of nutrient-deficient foods and fear is losing its capacity to function optimally. It is akin to a six cylinder engine functioning on only four cylinders. When assimilating holistic foods and living without fear, your body must truly respond to training with gratifying six cylinder results, the goal of this process.

Affirmation: I AM relaxing, releasing, and letting go of any preconceived ideas about what I think I know about dieting and applying these teachings. I ask to adopt holistic feedings and Rhythmic Training as a manner of living.

DAY SEVEN

REST	**COMMENTS**
Abdominals	

BUILDUP SHADE

Pink is symbolic of spirit, gentleness, and self-generosity. We are firmly, kindly, and gently building up the overall spirit of your health. From pale pink to hot pink, see which resonates most with your spirit. Each week of the Shade wear something pink at least once a week.

<u>WEEK THREE</u>

Sunday

Prime Compass

- Rhythmically training is an incandescent portal to adding years with grace and poise. Still your being, your entire body and mind, and listen to the Power you will use for strength throughout your training.

Affirmation: I AM continuing to the next Shade to get in the best shape of my life. I desire to live a long, healthy life marked by adding years with poise, strength, and grace.

DAY ONE

Exercise	Sets	Reps	Percentage	Rest	Comments
Warm-up and Stretching					
Front Squat	8	8	67%1RM	2 minute	

				s	
DB MilitaryPre ss	2	6	“		
Decline Abs.	2	6			
Chin-ups	2	6			
Kettlebell or DB Swings	3	30 second s		10 second s	

Monday
Continuance

- You are worthy of all that is healthy. Although this truth may sometimes be difficult for you to absorb, allow yourself to feel the love of this truth.
- Feeling this, you automatically speak and act in manners that move you ever nearer to holistic health. Breaking your previous thought and feeding patterns may be slow and requires continuance.

Affirmation: I AM acknowledging that I AM worth a healthier, more supple physique. I ask to remain positive mentally, physically, and spiritually as I pursue holistic harmony.

DAY TWO

Exercise	**Set s**	**Rep s**	**Percentag e**	**Rest**	**Comment s**
Warm-up and Stretching					

Abdominals: Inchworm	3	10		30 seconds	
***Cardio: 22 minutes**			Warm-up 5 minutes then Fast as possible @ Level 6-10 for 1 minute Recovery pace @ Level 3-5 for 2 minutes **Repeat 4 Times** Then Cool down		

*Sessions will consist of bike, stepper, elliptical, rowing, swimming, walking, stationary bike, treadmill, or any other cardiovascular activity.

Tuesday

Love

- I express enough love in my heart to follow this Rhythmic Training Dance commitment.
- I put Divine Love first; I honor my body in ways that reflect Divine Love. I fully treat and accept my body with compassion, kindness, and care.

- I take these words and check my thoughts, feelings, and actions.

Affirmation: I AM actively jumping the hurdles that once made me fearful and immobile. I AM lovingly moving on to meet my new body. I hope to maintain a loving attitude of continuing acceptance towards dancing through these Shades.

DAY THREE

Exercise	**Sets**	**Reps**	**Percentage**	**Rest**	**Comments**
Warm-up and Stretchin g					
Back Squat	5	6	67%1RM	3-5 min utes	
		5	75%1RM		
		5	80%1RM		
Abdomin als: Abs Wheel	1	12			

Wednesday
Choice

- You can choose to spend the rest of your life with a spring in your step and postural balance by applying purposeful training as your aging elixir. You may dislike training but, once you embark on this rhythmic voyage, you will be utterly satisfied you did.

➢ The choice of disciplining, commitment, and effort is totally up to you.

Affirmation: I AM unquestionably clear about the purpose and goal of my training and holistic dieting. I pray to sustain training that I may feast in better moods and foods for my mind and soul.

DAY FOUR

Exercise	**Sets**	**Reps**	**Percentage**	**Rest**	**Comments**
Warm-up and Stretching					
Abdominals: Crunches	2	15		30 seconds	
***Cardio: 22 minutes**			Warm-up 5 minutes then Fast as possible @ Level 6-10 for 1 minute Recovery pace @ Level 3-5 for 2 minutes **Repeat 4 Times** Then Cool down		

*Sessions will consist of bike, stepper, elliptical, rowing, swimming, walking, stationary bike, treadmill, or any other cardiovascular activity.

Thursday
Reduction

- Stand firm in your commitment! The correct development of your body can be a gem for increased mental power, longevity, and spiritual attainment.

Affirmation: I AM endeavoring to reduce the destructive elements in my life. I invite a new way of living and training to bring forth the best of my mind, body, and soul.

DAY FIVE

Exercise	**Sets**	**Reps**	**Percentage**	**Rest**	**Comments**
Warm-up and Stretching					
Cleans	4	6	65%1RM	3 minutes	
Abdominals: Planks	1	30 seconds hold			
Cardio: Brisk Walk **20 minutes**					

Friday
Eyes Up!

- Nutrient-deficient and vitamin-stripped food, ingesting in haste, insufficient exercise, and shallow breathing all are pathways to an irritable and pain-filled existence. Yet, by practical application of rhythmic training and simple nutrient-dense foods you can begin to improve and recover your vivid physical and mental condition.

Affirmation: I AM relaxing and releasing all objections, poisonous foods, and justifications for deterring my optimal health. I pray to cease turning a blind eye to what saturates my mind, body, and soul.

DAY SIX

Exercise	**Sets**	**Reps**	**Percentage**	**Rest**	**Comments**
Warm-up and Stretching					
Abdominals: Inchworm	3	12-15		30 seconds	
***Cardio: 30 minutes**			Steady-State @ 70 – 75% predicted maximum heart rate		

*Sessions will consist of bike, stepper, elliptical, rowing, swimming, walking, stationary bike, treadmill, or any out-door cardiovascular activity.

Saturday OFF
Changing?

- To impress upon you, whether you are aware of it, positive changes are already taking place within you. Simply by beginning to diet holistically and train, you have initiated positive forces and defused negative ones which operated for years.

Affirmation: I choose to continue changing and opening portals for smooth flowing internal relationships. I pray to relax, train, and have a beautiful day.

DAY SEVEN

REST	**COMMENTS**
Abdominals	

WEEK FOUR
Sunday
Patience

- Your patience is vital. Perchance you want quick results. Relax! Release! Let this restive

energy guide your inner reservoir for your training and spiritual support.

- Impatience can only fetter the progression process and distance you from your health milestones.

Affirmation: I AM trusting Spirit Force and continually strengthening my physique and my patience. I ask to practice patience, calmness, and strength when I become restive in my process of holistic health.

DAY ONE

Exercise	Sets	Reps	Percentage	Rest	Comments
Warm-up and Stretching					
Front Squat	8	8	67%1RM	2 minutes	
DB Military Press	2	6	"		
Decline Abs.	2	6			
Chin-ups	2	6	"		
Kettlebell or DB Swings	3	30 seconds		10 seconds	

Monday
Ego Puncture

- You are growing and rebuilding your spirit and body. To fully live rhythmically this dance, to rewardingly proceed along this path, requires that you train to the colorful reverberations of each session. It is only in the depth of the moment to moment training where the full awareness of the magic of you lives.

- The choice is yours, for taking advantage of all the opportunities for intimacy that these training tools offer.

Affirmation: I AM growing stronger and changing my attitudes as well as my physique. I pray to relax, release, and let go of my controlling ego and choose to view my training moments with a child-like receptiveness.

DAY TWO

Exercise	**Sets**	**Reps**	**Percentage**	**Rest**	**Comments**
Warm-up and Stretching					
Abdominals: Inchworm	3	12		30 seconds	
***Cardio: 22 minutes**			Warm-up 5 minutes then Fast as possible @ Level 6-10 for 1 minute Recovery pace @ Level 3-5 for 2		

			minutes **Repeat 4 Times** Then Cool down		

*Sessions will consist of bike, stepper, elliptical, rowing, swimming, walking, stationary bike, treadmill, or any other cardiovascular activity.

Tuesday
Firm Desire

- You are rhythmically training and reinforcing health, wholeness, and harmony. This process assures direction, definition, and desired days of firmness and vigor.

Affirmation: I AM standing firm on my training foundation and principles to support my health, wholeness, and harmony. I ask for the understanding and acceptance needed in my relationship with a holistic lifestyle.

DAY THREE

Exercise	Sets	Reps	Percentage	Rest	Comments
Warm-up and Stretching					
Back Squat	5	6	70%1RM	3-5 minutes	
		5	75%1RM		
		5	80%1RM		

Abdominals: Abs Wheel	1	15			

Wednesday
Rest

- Your commitment to experience periods of rest is crucial each day. Taking time to rest is an especially important element of your training day. It is in these quiet moments and hours that you fuel, feel, *restore, rejuvenate, and repair* completely your body's homoeostasis.
- Each night, as you rest physically, you also mentally and spiritually rest. Remember that prolonged periods of inadequate rest generate diminished returns.

Affirmation: I AM refreshing and restoring my body so that I can step back into the mainstream of my Training Dance with new strength. I pray to deliberately retreat and relax for many moments throughout my day.

DAY FOUR

Exercise	**Sets**	**Reps**	**Percentage**	**Rest**	**Comments**
Warm-up and Stretching					
Abdominals: Crunches	3	12		30 seconds	

***Cardio: 22 minutes**			Warm-up 5 minutes then Fast as possible @ Level 6-10 for 1 minute Recovery pace @ Level 3-5 for 2 minutes **Repeat 4 Times** Then Cool down		

*Sessions will consist of bike, stepper, elliptical, rowing, swimming, walking, stationary bike, treadmill, or any other cardiovascular activity.

Thursday
Being There Is Needed Most

- You are restoring your proper relationship with spirit, diet, and training. The natural beauties of your mind, body, and soul are inspired by your thoughtful choices and attitudes.
- The only terrible Training Dance sessions are the ones you refuse to show up for.

Affirmation: I AM training and dieting to accept self-discipline. I will cease letting myself passively bounce from diet to diet and from fear to fear. I choose to continue the structure and direction that comes with discovering the parameters of growth. And push me toward the goals which crowd my dreams.

DAY FIVE

Exercise	**Sets**	**Reps**	**Percentage**	**Rest**	**Comments**
Warm-up and Stretching					
Cleans	4	6	65%1RM	3 minutes	
Abdominals: Planks	2	20-30 seconds hold			
Cardio: Brisk Walk **20 minutes**					

Friday

The Necessary Foundation

➢ Being intent on your training is a necessary adjunct to a positively balanced soul and body. It will, no doubt, be able to guide your dieting and flexibility actions if you are prepared to accept its precepts; however, in no way can you expect optimal health if you turn your back on that support.

Affirmation: I AM willing to have years of clarity, mobility, stability, and joint integrity. I tender to remember: all that hinders my best health must be eliminated. It is up to me to make myself fit.

DAY SIX

Exercise	**Sets**	**Reps**	**Percentage**	**Rest**	**Comments**
Warm-up and Stretching					
Abdominals: Inchworm	3	12-15		25 seconds	
***Cardio: 30 minutes**			Steady-State @ 70 – 75% predicted maximum heart rate		

*Sessions will consist of bike, stepper, elliptical, rowing, swimming, walking, stationary bike, treadmill, or any out-door cardiovascular activity.

Saturday OFF

Divine Energy

- The Spirit Force within makes you equal to any challenge, strong enough to tread the toughest trail, wise enough to let go of stress, and loving enough to trust your ability to succeed.
- Divine Love flows through your entire body in a strengthening, repairing, and empowering stream of ***energy***.

Affirmation: I AM a child of Divine Love and through any challenge I AM never alone. I desire to believe I can flourish. I ask and know that always the spiritual strength of Spirit Force is with me.

DAY SEVEN

REST	**COMMENTS**
Abdominals	

<u>**WEEK FIVE**</u>

Sunday

Enthusiasm

- Rhythmic training is mental and physical, as well as soul constructive, for it is quite a well-known fact that scores of people have altered their health by practicing holistic dieting and training; other benefits are too numerous to mention.

Affirmation: I AM choosing to respond calmly yet enthusiastically to today's training. I ask my inner guide to help me continue in this unfamiliar way of dieting and training.

DAY ONE

Exercise	Sets	Reps	Percentage	Rest	Comments
Warm-up and Stretching					
Front Squat	8	8	67%1RM	2 minutes	
DB Military Press	2	6	"		
Decline Abs.	2	6			
Chin-ups	2	6	"		
Kettlebell or DB Swings	3	30 seconds		10 seconds	

Monday
Hope

➢ You know that it will rain after the drought, and you know that the darkness of the night is pursued by the light of dawn. You too have a radiant inner light—the most powerful light of all.

➢ Just as the light of the sun helps the plants, trees, and flowers grow and flourish, your inner light helps you grow and flourish. As you train, you are flourishing mentally, physically, and spiritually.

➢ The rhythmic training helps uncertainty dissolve from your mind, power and ***energy*** fill your body, and your health is rejuvenated.

➢ Your inner light radiates as a beacon of health, giving you the strength to train through any period of darkness.

Affirmation: I AM training through the darkness of my weaknesses by the power of my inner light. I resolve to value and trust my light as I clear away unhealthy dieting and fear and look with hope to the sessions ahead.

DAY TWO

Exercise	**Sets**	**Reps**	**Percentage**	**Rest**	**Comments**
Warm-up and Stretching					
Abdominals: Inchworm	3	15		30 seconds	
***Cardio: 22 minutes**			Warm-up 5 minutes		

			then Fast as possible @ Level 6-10 for 1 minute Recovery pace @ Level 3-5 for 2 minutes **Repeat 4 Times** Then Cool down		

*Sessions will consist of bike, stepper, elliptical, rowing, swimming, walking, stationary bike, treadmill, or any other cardiovascular activity.

Tuesday

Aging Grace

- You are building up an endowment in disposition, mobility, and *self-efficacy* that will give you more balance, lean tissue, and personal power as you add years. Training is your body's opportunity to play. Thus, be sure your attitude is positive as it influences your mind, body, and soul.

Affirmation: I AM keeping my mind, body, and soul in condition consistently so that the best may come to me. I desire to awaken and maintain a positive attitude for developing and preserving my physique's majesty.

DAY THREE

Exercise	**Sets**	**Reps**	**Percentage**	**Rest**	**Comments**
Warm-up and Stretching					
Back Squat	5	5	75%1RM	3-5 minutes	
		5	80%1RM		
		5	85%1RM		
Abdominals: Abs Wheel	1	15			

Wednesday

Unloading a Heavy Load

- Are you punishing your body by loading it with nutrient deficient foods? This lack of sustenance makes you eat more and still remain unsated.
- You must ingest enough calories and in a proper ratio.
- You must get enough sleep and rest. You are ruining yourself mentally and physically because your body nourishes your mind, and all movement is initiated by the mind.

Affirmation: I will cease being despairing. I no longer want to cause myself fruitless pain. I ask to see this training through with help from the Spirit Force.

DAY FOUR

Exercise	**Sets**	**Reps**	**Percentage**	**Rest**	**Comments**
Warm-up and Stretching					
Abdominals: Crunches	2	15		30 seconds	
***Cardio: 22 minutes**			Warm-up 5 minutes then Fast as possible @ Level 6-10 for 1 minute Recovery pace @ Level 3-5 for 2 minutes **Repeat 4 Times** Then Cool down		

*Sessions will consist of bike, stepper, elliptical, rowing, swimming, walking, stationary bike, treadmill, or any other cardiovascular activity.

Thursday
Willingness

- On the sound principles of Rhythmic Training I prepare for long-term healthy living. The adventure of living that kind of life and setting fitness goals is solidifying the foundation of my improved *self-efficacy.*

Affirmation: I AM open and willing to see this plan unfold in my health. I trust that the Omnipotent Force guides me in all my training activities.

DAY FIVE

Exercise	**Sets**	**Reps**	**Percentage**	**Rest**	**Comments**
Warm-up and Stretching					
Cleans	4	6	65%1RM	3 minutes	
Abdominals: Planks	3	20-30 seconds hold			

Friday
Trust

- The Training Dance strengthens your body session by session. Your body, in turn, enables you to live and move healthier.

➢ Focus your wholehearted attention on all the progress—seen and unseen. As you train, ask in a spirit of love and happiness for greater evidence of health. Trust the Spirit of Life within you to provide new physical strength and ***energy***.

Affirmation: I AM inspired and guided to reach my health milestones, knowing that success, too, is mine. I call for a new spiritual strength, that through the power of Spirit within, I AM able to feel truly healthier.

DAY SIX

Exercise	**Sets**	**Reps**	**Percentage**	**Rest**	**Comments**
Warm-up and Stretching					
Abdominals: Inchworm	3	12-15		25 seconds	
***Cardio: 35 minutes**			Steady-State @ 70 – 75% predicted maximum heart rate		

*Sessions will consist of bike, stepper, elliptical, rowing, swimming, walking, stationary bike, treadmill, or any out-door cardiovascular activity.

Saturday OFF
Breakers

- You can decide to see the Rhythmic Training Dance Shades as breakers—breakers that assist and support the tissue changes to manifest your spiritual and physical goals.
- Amid the Shade of each breaker, you sprout new strength, and the breaker to come will be more adroitly ridden.

Affirmation: I AM greeting the positive forces inherent in the breakers of progression. I choose to look upon the coming Shade as a surging breaker supporting my new sprouts of strength.

DAY SEVEN

REST	**COMMENTS**
Abdominals	

STRENGTH SHADE

Orange traditionally symbolizes power, adaptability, and stimulation. Orange makes you hungry. During the week, pay attention to where orange appears in the food industry.

<u>WEEK SIX</u>

Sunday

True Possession

- Health is the rarest of all possessions. It impresses upon your mind, body, and soul expression. By increasing your self-awareness, you can establish more control over your ***energy*** and actions.
- You are learning to move away from judging and toward accepting training. You can respond to holistic dieting as a calm, accepting friend. Once you unload the nutrient-deficient foods and fear your resolve will increase, and slowly your measurements will progressively decrease.

Affirmation: I AM re-committing to doing something delicious for myself every day. I pray to continue making healthier food and beverage choices, and embracing this strange and wonderful new ***energy.***

DAY ONE

Exercise	Sets	Reps	Percentage	Rest	Comments
Warm-up and Stretching					
Abdominals: Crunches	1	30			

***Cardio:** **25 minutes**			Warm-up 5 minutes then Fast as possible @ Level 6-10 for 1 minute Recovery pace @ Level 3-5 for 2 minutes **Repeat** **5 Times** Then Cool down		

*Sessions will consist of bike, stepper, elliptical, rowing, swimming, walking, stationary bike, treadmill, or any other cardiovascular activity.

Monday
Faith

- Faith is given to me in response to my prayers. It is a necessary weapon for me to possess for the overcoming of all adverse conditions and the accomplishing of success in living the Training Dance. Therefore I will have faith and work at strengthening my physique.

Affirmation: I AM learning to experience the peace of mind that is a result of rhythmic training. I desire to grow into an ongoing act of faith. I pray that I may follow that faith to victory in living my health goals.

DAY TWO

Exercise	Sets	Reps	Percentage	Rest	Comments
Warm-up and Stretching					
Front Squat	2	10	60%1RM	2 minutes	
Romanian Deadlift	2	10	"		
Single-leg Step-up	2	10	"		
Incline Bench Press	2	10	"		
Tricep Pulldown	2	10		1 minute	
Decline Abs	2	15		20-30 seconds	

Tuesday
Maintenance

➢ No one promised you body perfection, yesterday. Instead, the Training Dance Shades direct your process toward maintaining your functional integrity.

Affirmation: I AM learning to conserve ***energy*** by

training patiently. I pray, get out of the way, and show up for the development of this training day.

DAY THREE

Exercise	Sets	Reps	Percentage	Rest	Comments
Warm-up and Stretching					
Rack Clean	2	5	65%1RM	2 minutes	
High Pull	2	5	"		
Standing Shoulder Press	2	5	"		
Pull-ups	2		"		
Bicep E-Z Curl	2	10	"	1 minute	
Planks	2	20-30 seconds hold			

Wednesday

Rejuvenation

- The Rhythmic Training Dance leads your body to physiological rejuvenation. It is brought progressively from a state of latency to one of dynamic activity. This results in greatly improved health, added mental acuity, and greater spiritual and physical power.

Affirmation: I AM dancing and nourishing my body to be refined by a physiological rejuvenation, rendered through the intensity of my efforts. I make application by the constant practice of training based on sound physiology to give strength and vigor to my life.

DAY FOUR

Exercise	**Sets**	**Reps**	**Percentage**	**Rest**	**Comments**
Warm-up and Stretching					
Abdominals: Crunches	1	30			
***Cardio: 25 minutes**			Warm-up 5 minutes then Fast as possible @ Level 6-10 for 1 minute Recovery pace @ Level 3-5 for 2 minutes **Repeat 5 Times** Then Cool down		

*Sessions will consist of bike, stepper, elliptical,

rowing, swimming, walking, stationary bike, treadmill, or any other cardiovascular activity.

Thursday
Reality

- Your body is composed of numerous elements, and a deficiency of any one or more of these elements impairs the functioning of your entire system. An inadequate supply can be the major cause of a great many ailments. Therefore, it is imperative that your foods be ingested in the most natural state possible.

Affirmation: I AM living more the reality that ailments are unable to obtain traction when my body is in the best condition. I anticipate ingesting more whole foods and leafy vegetables as these contain those substances that my body must have to function optimally.

DAY FIVE

Exercise	**Sets**	**Reps**	**Percentage**	**Rest**	**Comments**
Warm-up and Stretching					
Front Squat	2	10	60%1RM	2 minutes	
Romanian Deadlift	2	10	"		
Single-leg Step-up	2	10	"		
Incline Bench Press	2	10	"		

Tricep Pulldown	2	10		1 minute	
Decline Abs	2	15		20-30 seconds	

Friday
Today

- You are now training and gaining the information, tools, and techniques to strengthen and maintain your physique and age more gracefully. Your willingness to adopt, develop, and sustain your training is directly related to your desire for improved *self-efficacy*.

Affirmation: I AM reinventing myself by choosing to consume the fruits of holistic living. I put forward the effort and apply these tools and techniques. Today!

DAY SIX

Exercise	**Sets**	**Reps**	**Percentage**	**Rest**	**Comments**
Warm-up and Stretchin g					
Rack Clean	2	5	65%1RM	2 min utes	
High Pull	2	5	"		
Standing Shoulder Press	2	5	"		
Pull-ups	2		"		
Bicep E-Z Curl	2	10		1 min	

				ute	
Planks	2	20-30 seconds hold			

Saturday OFF
Progression

- Your Training Dance Shades are gifts. They are hallmarks to your progression and readiness to grow.

Affirmation: I AM enjoying the challenges of dancing with the Shades to change my endurance, appearance, strength, and power. I request to lovingly grow in this progressive training process.

DAY SEVEN

REST	**COMMENTS**
Abdominals	

WEEK SEVEN

Sunday

"A Healthy Mind in a Healthy Body"

- In the beginning, you wanted to look fit and in shape first then train, but by now, you know this is a false premise. Then, you wanted to stay in shape and found keeping in shape is a matter of changing your lifestyle. It is that simple!
- Rhythmic Training facilitates you naturally stimulating your body without artificial, processed, and modified "additives."

Affirmation: I AM changing my attitude and outlook about fear, diet, and training. I will practice remembering it is more than calories in and calories out. Training is a necessity for those who seek to maintain a "healthy mind in a healthy body." I pray to stay in the stream of health in mind, body, and soul through this day.

DAY ONE

Exercise	Sets	Reps	Percentage	Rest	Comments
Warm-up and Stretching					
Abdominals: Crunches	1	30			
***Cardio: 25 minutes**			Warm-up 5 minutes then		

			Fast as possible @ Level 6-10 for 1 minute Recovery pace @ Level 3-5 for 2 minutes **Repeat 5 Times** Then Cool down		

*Sessions will consist of bike, stepper, elliptical, rowing, swimming, walking, stationary bike, treadmill, or any other cardiovascular activity.

Monday
Acceptance

- You must cease comparing your physique with those of others. How can you hope to measure up? Continue living the training dance, and focus on your assets and your faith.

Affirmation: I AM focusing and accepting with gratitude all that I AM. I desire to spend my ***energy*** adjusting, accepting, and applying myself to reach my health goals.

DAY TWO

Exercise	Sets	Reps	Percentage	Rest	Comments
Warm-up and Stretching					
Front Squat	3	10	65%1RM	2 minutes	
Romanian Deadlift	3	10	"		
Single-leg Step-up	3	10	"		
Incline Bench Press	3	10	"		
Tricep Pulldown	3	10		1 minute	
Decline Abs	3	15		20-30 seconds	

Tuesday

Overloading

- Just as dirty water in a glass can be replaced by pouring in clear water until the glass overflows, you can pour the clear water of encouraging words and acts of holistic dieting into your glass of rhythmic training. As you carefully pour out love, joy, and overload, you see your old physique being washed away.
-

Affirmation: I AM treading the upward path to greater physical and spiritual awareness. I AM in better understanding of my thoughts and my dieting and their relationship to Spirit. Patiently, I AM privileged to be witnessing a change occurring within them. Help me to change overeating to overloading.

DAY THREE

Exercise	Sets	Reps	Percentage	Rest	Comments
Warm-up and Stretchin g					
Rack Clean	3	5	70%1RM	2 minu tes	
High Pull	3	5	"		
Standing Shoulder Press	3	5	"		
Pull-ups	3		"		
Bicep E-Z Curl	3	10		1 minu te	
Planks	3	20-30 seco nds hold			

Wednesday

Salubrity

➢ Your goal of body harmony and salubrity is a special gift; it offers you mental, physical, and spiritual enhancement, provided you attend to the daily process as much as the goal.

Affirmation: I AM motivated to take positive advantage of this day's training. I AM excited about what I AM. In honesty I ask to allow the momentum of my health milestones to inspire me.

DAY FOUR

Exercise	Sets	Reps	Percentage	Rest	Comments
Warm-up and Stretching					
Abdominals: Crunches	1	30			
***Cardio: 25 minutes**			Warm-up 5 minutes then Fast as possible @ Level 6-10 for 1 minute Recovery pace @ Level 3-5 for 2 minutes **Repeat 5 Times** Then Cool down		

*Sessions will consist of bike, stepper, elliptical, rowing, swimming, walking, stationary bike, treadmill, or any other cardiovascular activity.

Thursday

Courage

- In a healthy manner, your weight issues and lethargy are powerfully transformed into a more self-confident you.
- You can prepare yourself by doing each day what you can to maintain and develop your wholeness. This preparation consists of holistic dieting, training reliably, and gradually gaining the power and ***energy*** you need.

Affirmation: I AM open to experiencing the vulnerability as well as the vitality rhythmically dancing through the training Shades offers. I desire to learn equally from the shadows, the shades, and the pain of courageously choosing to improve my health.

DAY FIVE

Exercise	**Sets**	**Reps**	**Percentage**	**Rest**	**Comments**
Warm-up and Stretching					
Front Squat	3	10	65%1RM	2 minutes	
Romanian Deadlift	3	10	"		
Single-leg Step-up	3	10	"		
Incline Bench Press	3	10	"		
	3	10		1 minute	
Decline	3	15		20-30	

Abs				seconds	

Friday
The Best

➢ Your positive attitude, your focus, and your willingness to train are manifesting themselves in desirable changes. You have gained an enhanced breath, mind, muscle, and soul connection to buoy you onward in your expedition.

Affirmation: I AM ultimately expressing the best of my mind, my body, and my soul. I pray to move through my training day, giving expression to my best.

DAY SIX

Exercise	**Sets**	**Reps**	**Percentage**	**Rest**	**Comments**
Warm-up and Stretching					
Rack Clean	3	5	70%1RM	2 minutes	
High Pull	3	5	"		
Standing Shoulder Press	3	5	"		
Pull-ups	3		"		
Bicep E-Z Curl	3	10		1 minute	
Planks	3	20-30 second			

		s hold			

Saturday OFF
Responsibility

- Your mind, body, and soul are so sacred. When combined, this is your true self, your best self.
- As you ponder this beloved truth, accept and appreciate that you must be sure to honor and respect it. In meeting your obligations and fulfilling your duties, you must be careful to keep all three optimally healthy.

Affirmation: I AM accepting responsibility and choosing to stay focused on training and expressing my best self. I ask to execute my commitment to dieting holistically without conditions and surrendering to my best self.

DAY SEVEN

REST Abdominals				**COMMENTS**	

WEEK EIGHT

Sunday

Slow and Thorough

- Gradually, you are building strength. You are accomplishing this in several ways. One way is by ingesting more nutrient-dense foods. You also build and strengthen your body by stretching and training. And finally, you strengthen your body by having and improving your mind-muscle connection.

Affirmation: I AM more aware of the subtle yet simultaneous influence of my mental, physical, and spiritual conditions. I ask that the specter of my wanting quick results as a solution dissipates.

DAY ONE

Exercise	Sets	Reps	Percentage	Rest	Comments
Warm-up and Stretching					
Abdominals: Crunches	1	30			
***Cardio: 25 minutes**			Warm-up 5 minutes then Fast as possible @ Level 6-10 for 1 minute		

			Recovery pace @ Level 3-5 for 2 minutes **Repeat 5 Times** Then Cool down		

*Sessions will consist of bike, stepper, elliptical, rowing, swimming, walking, stationary bike, treadmill, or any other cardiovascular activity.

Monday

Eustress

➢ You possess the ability to improve your diet, flexibility, spirit and strength by concerted effort. Beyond the obvious important role that rhythmically training your body plays in maintaining health, it is also a critically important method for your body to better disperse stress at the tissue level as well as environmentally.

Affirmation: I AM managing my health by empowering my body's innate ability to heal, adapt, and overcome. I trust that my concerted efforts will demonstrate optimal health.

DAY TWO

Exercise	Sets	Reps	Percentage	Rest	Comments
Warm-up and Stretching					
Front Squat	3	10	60%1RM	2 minutes	
Romanian Deadlift	3	10	"		
Single-leg Step-up	3	10	"		
Incline Bench Press	3	10	"		
	3	10		1 minute	
Decline Abs	3	15		20-30 seconds	

Tuesday
Breathing

- Your Rhythmic Training provides many invitations for deep breaths. Seize and embrace these opportunities to feel your inner power as well as your inner strength.
- Learn to engage your breathing as an invigoration window for sensing your progress and growth—the expedition of a healthier you.

Affirmation: I AM sated by the wealth of my breath and my wholeness mentally, physically, and spiritually in this moment. I pray to trust Spirit and know that I AM richly endowed. Now!

DAY THREE

Exercise	Sets	Reps	Percentage	Rest	Comments
Warm-up and Stretching					
Rack Clean	3	5	65%1RM	2 minutes	
High Pull	3	5	"		
Standing Shoulder Press	3	5	"		
Pull-ups	3		"		
Bicep E-Z Curl	3	10	"	1 minute	
Planks	3	20-30 seconds hold			

Wednesday
Simplicity

- You must be self-supportive and commit to cease sabotaging your efforts. As you practice this, you will tap into a needed source of inner ***energy*** that you can channel into attaining your body milestones.

Affirmation: I AM living the powerful simplicity of Rhythmic Training. I pray that the power of training will so invigorate me that I shall indeed walk on to the full physique harmony I seek.

DAY FOUR

Exercise	Sets	Reps	Percentage	Rest	Comments
Warm-up and Stretching					
Abdominals: Crunches	1	30			
***Cardio: 25 minutes**			Warm-up 5 minutes then Fast as possible @ Level 6-10 for 1 minute Recovery pace @ Level 3-5 for 2 minutes **Repeat 5 Times** Then Cool down		

*Sessions will consist of bike, stepper, elliptical, rowing, swimming, walking, stationary bike, treadmill, or any other cardiovascular activity.

Thursday
Power

- You are treading the trail of training, self-mastery, and self-control. At a level beyond what your senses tell you, you are Spirit.
- Nutrition-deficient foods, fear and subpar health have only as much control or power in your lives as you have given them.

Affirmation: I AM deciding to take control of my thoughts, my feelings and my actions. I desire to have confidence in Spirit, and give power only to positive thoughts and feelings today.

DAY FIVE

Exercise	Sets	Reps	Percentage	Rest	Comments
Warm-up and Stretching					
Front Squat	3	10	60%1RM	2 minutes	
Romanian Deadlift	3	10	"		
Single-leg Step-up	3	10	"		
Incline Bench Press	3	10	"		
	3	10		1 minute	
Decline Abs	3	15		20-30 seconds	

Friday
Love

- What an exquisite elation it is to know a sense of power and poise that reflects in your training interactively! You are opening the channels of Divine Love in countless ways. Likened to seeing the sun rising in brilliant glory or watching the sprouting of new life in the spring, there is a loving power working as you experience the interactions of holistic dieting and the Training Dance.
- You are touched and aware of the rejuvenating power that pervades your mind and body, the inspiring power that touches your spirit and keeps you serene through stressful days.

Affirmation: I AM more aware of Divine Love within and around me today. I tender with a spirit of service as I weave the common threads of training and nurturing myself mentally, physically, and spiritually.

DAY SIX

Exercise	**Sets**	**Reps**	**Percentage**	**Rest**	**Comments**
Warm-Up And Stretching					
Rack Clean	3	5	65%1rm	2 Minutes	
High Pull	3	5	"		
Standing Shoulder Press	3	5	"		
Pull-Ups	3		"		

Bicep E-Z Curl	3	10		1 Minute	
Planks	3	20-30 Seconds Hold			

Saturday OFF

Respect

- Your beginning to train was your willingness to take action. As you exert yourself to dance with the Shades of training, you discern a power that gives you the ability to continue dancing. By respecting your physique and caring for its natural ability to heal and grow, it is strengthened, and your attitude and *self-efficacy* are empowered.

Affirmation: I AM learning to think differently and train through tranquility or travail. I put forward that the joy of dancing with the Shades for optimal health shall be mine in full measure.

DAY SEVEN

REST Abdominals				**COMMENTS**	

WEEK NINE

Sunday

Clarity

- You may slide into previous feeding behaviors and fears, losing sight of your goal due to emotional upsets. Remember: recovery, rejuvenation, return is the Training Dance process—one which rebuilds, redefines, and reinstates holistic living by relaxing, releasing, and letting go.

Affirmation: I AM emerging like a beautiful flower as I give my body its proper nutrition. I pray to tread the path of commitment, and express myself positively.

DAY ONE

Exercise	Sets	Reps	Percentage	Rest	Comments
Warm-up and Stretching					
Abdominals: Crunches	1	30			
***Cardio: 28 minutes**			Warm-up 5 minutes then Fast as possible @ Level 6-10 for 1 minute Recovery		

			pace @ Level 3-5 for 2 minutes **Repeat 6 Times** Then Cool down		

*Sessions will consist of bike, stepper, elliptical, rowing, swimming, walking, stationary bike, treadmill, or any other cardiovascular activity.

Monday
Listening

- Listening is communication. Do you listen to your body? Your Circulation? Your Skin? Your Essence?
- When you speak to yourself, it is essential that you also listen to the Divine presence within you. Albeit this voice is inaudible, you know that the Divine speaks to you through your feeling nature and your intuition. It is essential for you to take time to quiet your innermost thoughts so that you can hear what the Divine Spark "speaks" to you.

Affirmation: I AM poised for positive and optimistic listening this training day. I pray that my words, unspoken and spoken, are uplifting.

DAY TWO

Exercise	Sets	Reps	Percentage	Rest	Comments
Warm-up and Stretching					
Front Squat	3	10	70%1RM	2 minutes	
Romanian Deadlift	3	10	"		
Single-leg Step-up	3	10	"		
Incline Bench Press	3	10	"		
	3	10		1 minute	
Decline Abs	3	15		20-30 seconds	

Tuesday

Passion

➢ There are two constant relationships. Your relationship with Spirit, which is required to fill you with peace in times of turmoil and inspire you in times of indecision, and your relationship with food. Situations in your life may change, but your body's requirements for nutrients are relatively constant.

➢ Each of these relationships are required to support you to live, play, work, and rest each day with a new eagerness and a new commitment—

and to allow you to experience these challenges in the best of health.

Affirmation: I AM grateful for the strength to face any training day and external change with inner peace and preparedness. I hope for passion, patience, compassion, and laughter–these are some of the many spiritual gifts that God has given me–as I train and maintain my relationship with body, mind, and soul.

DAY THREE

Exercise	**Sets**	**Reps**	**Percentage**	**Rest**	**Comments**
Warm-up and Stretching					
Rack Clean	3	5	75%1RM	2 minutes	
High Pull	3	5	"		
Standing Shoulder Press	3	5	"		
Pull-ups	3		"		
Bicep E-Z Curl	3	10		1 minute	
Planks	3	20-30 seconds hold			

Wednesday

Power

➢ For each session you attend, congratulate yourself. You will begin to feel more and more comfortable in doing things that you need to do, but would really rather be doing something else. You are enhancing your *self-efficacy*, which is a key element in the Rhythmic Training formula.

Affirmation: I AM enhancing my *self-efficacy* with strong, solid, and supportive words and actions. I propose to change my dieting behavior session by session knowing that each adds power to living healthier.

DAY FOUR

Exercise	**Sets**	**Reps**	**Percentage**	**Rest**	**Comments**
Warm-up and Stretching					
Abdominals: Crunches	1	30			
***Cardio: 28 minutes**			Warm-up 5 minutes then Fast as possible @ Level 6-10 for 1 minute Recovery pace @ Level 3-5 for 2 minutes **Repeat 6 Times** Then Cool down		

*Sessions will consist of bike, stepper, elliptical, rowing, swimming, walking, stationary bike, treadmill, or any other cardiovascular activity

Thursday
Joy

- Your fear-free holistic lifestyle will be a lifelong endeavor. Fortunately, you are on your unique expedition, and patience is a quality that will pay handsomely.

Affirmation: I AM patiently broadening my horizons for a longer life of fear-free thinking, independent mobility, and spinal integrity. I choose to be patient and full of unbridled joy as my body is being carefully orchestrated. Today!

DAY FIVE

Exercise	Sets	Reps	Percentage	Rest	Comments
Warm-up and Stretching					
Front Squat	3	10	70%1RM	2 minutes	
Romanian Deadlift	3	10	"		
Single-leg Step-up	3	10	"		
Incline Bench Press	3	10	"		
	3	10		1 minute	
Decline Abs	3	15		20-30 seconds	

Friday

Dedication

- The Rhythmic Training Dance institutes a gradual regimen to reduce corpulence and uneasiness and bring back a more natural physiology of health.

Affirmation: I AM bidding farewell to corpulence and uneasiness and instead dieting with love, patience, and dedication. I pray to continue training and restoring my natural health.

DAY SIX

Exercise	**Sets**	**Reps**	**Percentage**	**Rest**	**Comments**
Warm-up and Stretching					
Rack Clean	3	5	75%1RM	2 minutes	
High Pull	3	5	"		
Standing Shoulder Press	3	5	"		
Pull-ups	3		"		
Bicep E-Z Curl	3	10		1 minute	
Planks	3	20-30 seconds hold			

Saturday OFF

Pursuance

- You are the only person that can initiate and uphold the necessary change that will improve your health and influence your *self-efficacy*. Never suffocate yourself. Dare to continue with your physique agenda.

Affirmation: I AM quiet enough, for long enough, to be aware of the direction to go. I will confidently pursue my health agenda by moving further away from discarded fear and old feeding habits into the next Shade.

DAY SEVEN

REST	**COMMENTS**
Abdominals	

HIGH INTENSITY SHADE

Blue, in its lighter tones, represents inspiration and devotion, and both will be tested during this Shade. The deeper, vivid blues represent progress, successful enterprise, and laughter—all of which will expedite your obtaining your desired outcomes.

Be creative. As you train, think about the location and sounds of the blue ***energy***. Open up and give in to the relaxing sense that life is an alpha omega process with your inner self.

Pay attention to the different tones of blue: pearl, aquamarine, cyan, sapphire, and lapis to name a few, and allow their ***energies*** to impact and inspire you as needed.

WEEK TEN

Sunday

Transient Discomfort

- You have learnt increasing the resistance heightens the intensity of your results. Accepting these opportunities for progress, for increased strength, for increased self-awareness, offers you challenges of growth and preservation.

Affirmation: I AM trusting that transient discomforts guarantee me eased mobility, fluidity, and vitality. I approach this new Shade as a strange bounty insuring my strength and growth; without increased resistance and growth I atrophy and wither.

DAY ONE

Exercise	**Sets**	**Reps**	**Percentage**	**Rest**	**Comments**
Warm-up and Stretching					
Abdominals: Walking knee Lifts	1	12-15			
****Cardio: 30-45 minutes**			†Steady-State @ 70 – 75% predicted maximum heart rate with Interval Training break		

**10-20 minutes of steady-state (bike, stepper, treadmill or out-door running, cycling).

20-30 minutes of Interval Training. Break sessions up with steady-state warm-up and cool down.

†Interval Treadmill example: After a five minute warm-up, initiate 10-15 minutes of steady-state walking (0-3% grade @ 3.0-3.5 KPH/MPH); then move treadmill to 15% grade and adjust the speed to a level where you're walking @ a VERY brisk pace. Walk for 15 seconds then step on side rails for 30 seconds. Repeat for 20 minutes, and then finish with a five minute cool down. If you decide to increase the work time, try to keep the rest ration at

exactly twice the time you spend working.

Monday
Functional Risks

- Your DOMS (delayed onslaught muscle soreness) can serve as proof of what is taking place within you. To experience all that each Shade teaches you, your entire physique must be transformed.
- In spite of appearances, positive changes are taking place. The signs of external changes begin within at the cellular level.

Affirmation: I AM dancing forward in my training, trusting that each day adds mobility and stability to my functional health. I ask to dare taking the risks and so advance to greater *self-efficacy* and expressions of health.

DAY TWO

Exercise	**Sets**	**Reps**	**Percentage**	**Rest**	**Comments**
Warm-up and Stretching					
Deadlift (DL)	3	5	70%1RM	3 minutes	
Romanian (DL)	3	5	"		
45º Lunge	3	5	"		
Incline Bench Press	3	5	"		
Dips	3	5			
Side Bends Abs	2	15		20-30 seconds	

Tuesday

Change

- Changing your dieting—being aware, being alert, and being responsible—is pertinent.
- You are changing your activity levels and being aware of the amazing demonstrations of increased ***energy.***
- You are changing your thoughts and feelings to protect them and to keep negativity or doubt from growing there. As you change your dieting, you experience stress solutions as well as physical ones.

Affirmation: I AM focused, and I expect beautiful, bright tomorrows for my health. I ask to embrace change more freely and enthusiastically. Today!

DAY THREE

Exercise	Sets	Reps	Percentage	Rest	Comments
Warm-up and Stretching					
Hang Clean	3	5	75%1RM	3 minutes	
Push Press	3	5	"		
Standing Low Row	3	5	"		
Neutral Grip Pull ups	3	5			
Hand Planks	2	20-30 seconds hold			

Wednesday
Faith

- Is fear replacing Love in your body? It is said that fear is unable to exist where there is faith.
- Your body is an intriguing interdependent ***energy*** system. Reflect and revere the interplay between the Love that created you, your inner strength, and the powerful ***energy*** of each.

Affirmation: I AM letting my faith direct my every training and dieting action. I pray to remember that my faith and my training, like any skill, will decompose with lack of use.

DAY FOUR

Exercise	**Sets**	**Reps**	**Percentage**	**Rest**	**Comments**
Warm-up and Stretching					
Abdominals: Walking knee Lifts	1	12-15			
****Cardio: 30-45 minutes**			† Steady-State @ 70 – 75% predicted maximum heart rate with		

			Interval Training break		

**10-20 minutes of steady-state (bike, stepper, treadmill or out-door running, cycling).

20-30 minutes of Interval Training. Break sessions up with steady-state warm-up and cool down.

†Interval Treadmill example: After a five minute warm-up, initiate 10-15 minutes of steady-state walking (0-3% grade @ 3.0-3.5 KPH/MPH); then move treadmill to 15% grade and adjust the speed to a level where you're walking @ a VERY brisk pace. Walk for 15 seconds then step on side rails for 30 seconds. Repeat for 20 minutes, and then finish with a five minute cool down. If you decide to increase the work time, try to keep the rest ration at exactly twice the time you spend working.

Thursday
Surrender

- You in all probability discover relative ease in surrendering to the things you like. Can you gracefully surrender to the changing attitudes, actions, and beliefs desired for living the Training Dance and growing in lean body mass?

Affirmation: I AM re-surrendering my personal resistance and opening the portal to more love, and more health. I ask for a deeper awakening to the joys of owning a sharper mind, a leaner body, and a freer soul.

DAY FIVE

Exercise	Sets	Reps	Percentage	Rest	Comments
Warm-up and Stretching					
Back Squat	3	5	75%1RM	3-4 minutes	
Romanian DL	3	5	"		
Inline Lunge	3	5	"		
Bench Press	3	5	"		
Dips	3	5			
Side Bend Abs	2	15		20-30 seconds	

Friday
Honor

- You must choose to assert a measure of control over your physique as well as your brain. Once this discipline is gained, you can live being excited about your personal beauty and inspired by actively living your training.

Affirmation: I AM daring to let my mental, physical, and spiritual beauty reign by choosing to rhythmically train. I desire to unconditionally develop and honor myself mentally, physically, and spiritually.

DAY SIX

Exercise	Sets	Reps	Percentage	Rest	Comments
Warm-up and Stretching					
Hang Clean	3	5	75%1RM	3 minutes	
Push Press	3	5	"		
Standing Low Row	3	5	"		
Neutral Grip Pull ups	3	5			
Hand Planks	2	20-30 seconds hold			

Saturday OFF
Discovery

- As you begin to live the confidence and the comfort of your healthy *self-efficacy*, you are conveying the best in yourself. So today, in celebration of you, do one small thing for another soul who will never be able to reimburse you.

Affirmation: I AM discovering that my optimal health is made up of many little things. I will continue developing a healthy, loving attitude toward myself and others without **O**bligations, **J**udgments, **E**xpectations, **C**onditions.

DAY SEVEN

REST	**COMMENTS**
Abdominals	

WEEK ELEVEN

Sunday

Patience

- While grasping Rhythmic Training and holistic dieting your carefulness is paramount, for excess weight and a lightly active lifestyle will take more than a twinkling to transform. So practice the Shades to enjoy fullness of your mind, body, and soul.
- Never proceed to the point of intense strain. Your salubrity is unconquerable by strain, but only by patience and persistence. Regardless of how difficult an exercise seems, try it as best as you can and keep trying daily, making a little improvement each session, but never strain beyond your capacity.

Affirmation: I AM remodeling my body, for mind, soul, and body are interdependent, so that when the latter is regulated, so is the mind. I seek to quiet my body, soul, and mind through patient dancing with the Shades.

DAY ONE

EXERCISE	SETS	REPS	PERCENTAGE	REST	COMMENTS
Warm-up and Stretching					
Abdominals: Walking knee Lifts		15			
****Cardio: 30-45 minutes**			† Steady-State @ 70 – 75% predicted maximum heart rate with Interval Training break		

**10-20 minutes of steady-state (bike, stepper, treadmill or out-door running, cycling).

20-30 minutes of Interval Training. Break sessions up with steady-state warm-up and cool down.

†Interval Treadmill example: After a five minute warm-up, initiate 10-15 minutes of steady-state walking

(0-3% grade @ 3.0-3.5 KPH/MPH); then move treadmill to 15% grade and adjust the speed to a level where you're walking @ a VERY brisk pace. Walk for 15 seconds then step on side rails for 30 seconds. Repeat for 20 minutes, and then finish with a five minute cool down. If you decide to increase the work time, try to keep the rest ration at exactly twice the time you spend working.

Monday

Power

- Getting started can be the most difficult part of your training day. Control of your breathing controls your physical state. So relax, smile, and think about your milestone reward.
- You can breathe in and enjoy your source of power and know, every time you take a step towards your physique goal, you are taking a risk, and without the risk there can be no reward. So risk it all for the physique harmony you seek.

Affirmation: I AM breathing in partnership with the eternal source of power within and building the health I desire. I request the physical and spiritual power to risk listening internally and training, again and again, to own the physique I deserve.

DAY TWO

Exercise	Sets	Reps	Percentage	Rest	Comments
Warm-up and Stretching					
Deadlift (DL)	3	5	75%1RM	3 minutes	
Romanian (DL)	3	5	"		
45^{0} Lunge	3	5	"		
Incline Bench Press	3	5	"		
Dips	3	5			
Side Bends Abs	3	15		20-30 seconds	

Tuesday
Intensity

- Your rhythmic training is a means to concentration, your mind substance is still and rendered calm, and then its ***energies*** may be focused to a certain point. Your brain focus becomes the current of your body, and you gain power for more intensity.

Affirmation: I AM fully present for all the demands, changes, and opportunities of wholeness offered by this training day. I inhale deeply and pray to live more fully, the whole ***energy*** of human and divine in my body.

DAY THREE

Exercise	Sets	Reps	Percentage	Rest	Comments
Warm-up and Stretching					
Hang Clean	3	5	80%1RM	3 minutes	
Push Press	3	5	"		
Standing Low Row	3	5	"		
Neutral Grip Pull ups	3	5			
Hand Planks	3	30-45 seconds hold			

Wednesday
Vibrant Living

- Do you want to be optimally healthy?
- In order to be your healthiest, you are learning to do what is best. From the seemingly most significant part of the Training Dance to the seemingly most menial. You are changing your thoughts and your diet as well as building your mobility and your strength.

Affirmation: I AM lovingly reminding myself to stay on track, to keep focused on all facets of my living healthier. I inspire to live the vibrancy involved in all aspects of my training dance.

DAY FOUR

Exercise	Sets	Reps	Percentage	Rest	Comments
Warm-up and Stretching					
Abdominals: Walking knee Lifts	1	15			
****Cardio: 30-45 minutes**			† Steady-State @ 70 – 75% predicted maximum heart rate with Interval Training break		

**10-20 minutes of steady-state (bike, stepper, treadmill or out-door running, cycling).

20-30 minutes of Interval Training. Break sessions up with steady-state warm-up and cool down.

†Interval Treadmill example: After a five minute warm-up, initiate 10-15 minutes of steady-state walking (0-3% grade @ 3.0-3.5 KPH/MPH); then move treadmill to 15% grade and adjust the speed to a level where you're walking @ a VERY brisk pace. Walk for 15 seconds then step on side rails for 30 seconds. Repeat for 20 minutes, and then finish with a five minute cool down. If you decide

to increase the work time, try to keep the rest ration at exactly twice the time you spend working.

Exercise	Sets	Reps	Percentage	Rest	Comments
Warm-up and Stretching					
Abdominals					
Cardio					

Thursday

Purpose

- What has fear, overeating, or ingesting processed food stuff have that Rhythmic Training and holistic dieting lack? Are you open to believing that the liabilities of the former outweigh the assets?

Affirmation: I AM enthusiastically moving forward to achieve my training goals. I AM releasing anything and everything that no longer serves my purpose. I ask that I may strengthen myself spiritually, structurally, and functionally so that I may enjoy healthier postural and movement patterns. I ask that my body may be restored in suppleness and grace.

DAY FIVE

Exercise	Sets	Reps	Percentage	Rest	Comments
Warm-up and Stretching					
Back Squat	3	5	80%1RM	3-4 minutes	
Romanian DL	3	5	"		
Inline Lunge	3	5	"		
Bench Press	3	5	"		
Dips	3	5			
Side Bend Abs	3	15		20-30 seconds	

Friday

Au Natural

- To practice the Training Dance, you must practice the will to bear discomfort. The fact that the older one grows, the more aches and pains become part of daily living, can be drastically reduced by your willingness to practice the Training Dance and bear its fruitful, transient discomforts.
- Therefore, to age more gracefully, train, replete, rest, and repeat in lieu of reaching for pills. Choose your aches and pains—train the muscles.

Affirmation: I AM reminding myself that resistance training is the only natural stimulus that causes increases in lean tissue. I ask to train that I may complain less about fruitless pains. Now!

DAY SIX

Exercise	Sets	Reps	Percentage	Rest	Comments
Warm-up and Stretching					
Hang Clean	3	5	80%1RM	3 minutes	
Push Press	3	5	"		
Standing Low Row	3	5	"		
Neutral Grip Pull ups	3	5			
Hand Planks	3	30-45 seconds hold			

Saturday OFF

Honesty and Continuance

➢ Spirit of Truth, many times I have begun dieting and initiating a healthier, fear-free lifestyle and for some reason or another I never continue? Why? Why is it that I permit myself to be distracted from what I say I want to accomplish?

➢ Your discipline in following the Training Dance can be hindered by fear of failure, but this fear can be surrendered by a change of attitude, which you absolutely dominate.

Affirmation: I AM rededicating myself now, Spirit of Truth, to following this holistic dieting, to surrender myself totally to this guidance. I request the fortitude to finish what I have started and the ability to feel worthy of a healthier, sexier, more harmonious physique.

DAY SEVEN

REST	**COMMENTS**
Abdominals	

WEEK TWELVE

Sunday

Intensity Increase

- Your fears congeal your life. Real or imagined, they will be dissipated solely by your steady training actions.
- You can ease into increased intensities. They are your allies, and their presence invites prolonged mobility, stability, and vigor.

Affirmation: I AM reminding myself over and over again—day in and day out—follow the dance and keep an open mind. I pray to release my fear and the comfort of sameness and risk embracing the opportunities for new growth.

DAY ONE

Exercise	Sets	Reps	Percentage	Rest	Comments
Warm-up and Stretching					
Abdominals: Walking knee Lifts	1	15-20			
****Cardio: 30-45 minutes**			† Steady-State @ 70 – 75% predicted maximum heart rate with Interval Training break		

**10-20 minutes of steady-state (bike, stepper, treadmill or out-door running, cycling).

20-30 minutes of Interval Training. Break sessions up with steady-state warm-up and cool down.

†Interval Treadmill example: After a five minute warm-up, initiate 10-15 minutes of steady-state walking (0-3% grade @ 3.0-3.5 KPH/MPH); then move treadmill to 15% grade and adjust the speed to a level where you're walking @ a VERY brisk pace. Walk for 15 seconds then step on side rails for 30 seconds. Repeat for 20 minutes, and then finish with a five minute cool down. If you decide

to increase the work time, try to keep the rest ration at exactly twice the time you spend working.

Monday
Overfatness

- Your diligence and your partnership with the Divine Principle will facilitate your chiseling away the unnecessary fat as your new form emerges from within.
- Your vision for your body is worth rhythmically flowing with the music of the Training Dance day by day, Shade by Shade.

Affirmation: I AM thanking the Divine for releasing me from the painfulness of fear and excess weight pressing down on my joints. I pray to twirl across the days ahead and feel deeply my blossoming shades of beauty.

DAY TWO

Exercise	**Sets**	**Reps**	**Percentage**	**Rest**	**Comments**
Warm-up and Stretching					
Deadlift (DL)	2	5	50%1RM	2 minutes	
Kettlebell or DB Abs.	3	15		20-30 seconds	

Tuesday
Humility

- By training and practicing holistic dieting, I have a closer relationship with Spirit Force. I AM blessed to know the truth that with Spirit Force, all things are possible.
- I have learned to relax, release, and let go of outer concerns and to have confidence in Spirit as my source of direction and blessings. I have also learned that my body is my place of safety, healing, and rejuvenation.
- The Rhythmic Training teaches me to explore my strength, to heighten my spirituality, and to develop my body to its full potential.
- Training reminds me to have a greater awareness of the divinity in me. It assists me to access more the power within the human form.

Affirmation: I AM guided and my strength is supported by following the trail to body harmony and beauty. I ask to think, to diet, and to train in the flow of the all-powerful Spirit.

DAY THREE

Exercise	Sets	Reps	Percentage	Rest	Comments
Warm-up and Stretching					
Deadlift (DL)	2	5	75%1RM	3 minutes	
Kettlebell or DB	3	30		45 seconds	

Abs.					

Wednesday

Honesty

- How am I living? Am I Healthy? Joyful? Happy? Do I enjoy the beauty around and within me?
- I can gain a new way of living through prayer, training, and holistic dieting.
- Prayer invigorates my awareness of Spirit. This stimulated awareness fortifies all areas of my life. I can express joy more fully. I feel a better sense of well-being. I have a heightened appreciation of the beauty around and within me.

Affirmation: I AM alive in Spirit. I AM alive with the joy of healthy living—physically, mentally, and spiritually. I ask that whenever I feel out of touch during the day, I call forth this affirmation that I may feel the Grace that surrounds me.

DAY FOUR

Exercise	Sets	Reps	Percentage	Rest	Comments
Warm-up and Stretching					
Abdominals: Walking knee Lifts	1	15-20			
****Cardio: 30-45 minutes**			† Steady-State @ 70 –		

			75% predicted maximum heart rate with Interval Training break		

**10-20 minutes of steady-state (bike, stepper, treadmill or out-door running, cycling).

20-30 minutes of Interval Training. Break sessions up with steady-state warm-up and cool down.

†Interval Treadmill example: After a five minute warm-up, initiate 10-15 minutes of steady-state walking (0-3% grade @ 3.0-3.5 KPH/MPH); then move treadmill to 15% grade and adjust the speed to a level where you're walking @ a VERY brisk pace. Walk for 15 seconds then step on side rails for 30 seconds. Repeat for 20 minutes, and then finish with a five minute cool down. If you decide to increase the work time, try to keep the rest ration at exactly twice the time you spend working.

Exercise	**Sets**	**Reps**	**Percentage**	**Rest**	**Comments**
Warm-up and Stretching					
Abdominals					
Light Cardio					

Thursday

Combined Power

- By rhythmically training you can use meditation, weight, friction, and gravity to gain innumerable results. Physical power and health comes from training just as spirit-power comes from communicating with Spirit in quiet meditation. Your combining the two greatly assists you in attaining physique harmony and beauty.

Affirmation: I choose to remember that the power within me is greater than any task, for I AM on a positive path. I ask that I may be able to reach my health goals by continuing to combine these powers.

DAY FIVE

Exercise	Sets	Reps	Percentage	Rest	Comments
Warm-up and Stretching					
Rack Cleans	2	5	50%1RM	2 minutes	
Kettlebell or DB Abs.	3	15		20-30 seconds	

Friday

Self Endorsement

- Your current choice to train makes your unique contributions to approaching the richness of your own unfolding of harmoniously living healthier in your body.

- Today may be one wherein you think you lack the strength, then again ask Spirit Force for any strength and motivation you require.

Affirmation: I AM daring to fully live, discover, and endorse my sexy self. Today I ask for a richer *self-efficacy* and well-being.

DAY SIX

Exercise	Sets	Reps	Percentage	Rest	Comments
Warm-up and Stretching					
Deadlift (DL)	2	5	65%1RM	2 minutes	
Kettlebell or DB Abs.	3	30	"	45 seconds	

Saturday OFF
Love

- Through training, listening, and observing, you undoubtedly are learning that maintenance of your health is a lifelong expedition. So just for today you will live "in love" with the ***energy*** that is you—feel it, think it, be it.

Affirmation: I AM content with all that I AM. Now! I ask to bask in the ***energy*** from which I was created—Love.

DAY SEVEN

REST	**COMMENTS**
Abdominals	

WEEK THIRTEEN

Sunday

Heightened Intensity

- Conquering new intensities invites you to grow, to shift gears, and venture beyond your zone of comfort. They create the inner environment for you to have the physique you dream of.

Affirmation: I AM letting go of any fears and inviting a cascade of peace, health, and harmony to take its place. I ask to live fully in the moments of today's session with gratitude for all I hear, see, feel, touch, taste, and smell.

DAY ONE

Exercise	Sets	Reps	Percentage	Rest	Comments
Warm-up and Stretching					
Abdominals: Walking knee Lifts	1	20			
****Cardio:**					

30-45 minutes			† Steady-State @ 70 – 75% predicted maximum heart rate with Interval Training break		

**10-20 minutes of steady-state (bike, stepper, treadmill or out-door running, cycling)

20-30 minutes of Interval Training. Break sessions up with steady-state warm-up and cool down.

†Interval Treadmill example: After a five minute warm-up, initiate 10-15 minutes of steady-state walking (0-3% grade @ 3.0-3.5 KPH/MPH); then move treadmill to 15% grade and adjust the speed to a level where you're walking @ a VERY brisk pace. Walk for 15 seconds then step on side rails for 30 seconds. Repeat for 20 minutes, and then finish with a five minute cool down. If you decide to increase the work time, try to keep the rest ration at exactly twice the time you spend working.

Monday

Fiery Conviction

- Through your training and an inner connection with your spiritual self, your desired results unfold. With each new training day and each new Shade, your healthy life becomes clearer.

➢

Affirmation: I AM treading forward with conviction. I know where I AM going! I ask to implement my plan and purpose of healthier living.

DAY TWO

Exercise	Sets	Reps	Percentage	Rest	Comments
Warm-up and Stretching					
Deadlift (DL)	3	5	80%1RM	4 minutes	
Romanian (DL)	3	5	"		
45⁰ Lunge	3	5	"		
Incline Bench Press	3	5	"		
Dips	3	5			
Side Bends Abs	3	30		20-30 seconds	

Tuesday

Thirsty?

➢ Your desire for a better physique is genuine. Knowing this, you must choose to act in caring ways that radiate loving-kindness in its maintenance.

➢ Rhythmically training is akin to your ingesting a long, cool drink of water in the hottest desert. You quench a thirst for fluid mobility as well as your mental, physical, and spiritual longevity. How deep is your thirst for physical health, harmony, and beauty?

Affirmation: I AM quietly affirming my desire for, and readiness to, quench this thirst for a healthier self. I ask to be whole in thought and dedication, whole in mind and body, whole in spirit, speech, and action.

DAY THREE

Exercise	**Sets**	**Reps**	**Percentage**	**Rest**	**Comments**
Warm-up and Stretching					
Hang Clean	3	5	85%1RM	4 minutes	
Push Press	3	5	"		
Standing Low Row	3	5	"		
Neutral Grip Pull ups	3	5			
Hand Planks	3	45 seconds hold			

Wednesday
Seizing Today

- It is at Shade's end when your milestone is in sight, that your nerves and heart, and muscles and motivation are strained almost to the threshold.

- You are learning to respond in a constructive manner to the destructive influences that may arise in holistic living. Are you entertaining fantasies and expectations? Stay in the present. Relax, own and enjoy the moments, today.

Affirmation: I AM maintaining an atmosphere of discovery. I pray to learn to take the necessary actions today and trust Spirit.

DAY FOUR

Exercise	**Sets**	**Reps**	**Percentage**	**Rest**	**Comments**
Warm-up and Stretching					
Abdominals: Walking knee Lifts	1	20			
****Cardio: 30-45 minutes**			† Steady-State @ 70 – 75% predicted maximum heart rate with Interval Training break		

**10-20 minutes of steady-state (bike, stepper, treadmill or out-door running, cycling)

20-30 minutes of Interval Training. Break sessions up with steady-state warm-up and cool down.

†Interval Treadmill example: After a five minute warm-up, initiate 10-15 minutes of steady-state walking (0-3% grade @ 3.0-3.5 KPH/MPH); then move treadmill to 15% grade and adjust the speed to a level where you're walking @ a VERY brisk pace. Walk for 15 seconds then step on side rails for 30 seconds. Repeat for 20 minutes, and then finish with a five minute cool down. If you decide to increase the work time, try to keep the rest ration at exactly twice the time you spend working.

Exercise	**Sets**	**Reps**	**Percentage**	**Rest**	**Comments**
Warm-up and Stretching					
Abdominals					
Cardio					

Thursday

Choice

➢ Often times, the effort to rise above the old patterns of living appears to be more than you can handle, and you may choose to remain stagnated. For a time, you may even feel safe there.

➢ Ultimately, however, the stagnation will cease being enough to satisfy your deeper longings. Then it is time you extend beyond your fears and move forward.

➢ As you emerge from the stagnation, you can rise above your fears and look ahead to the blessings in store for you.

➢ Remember, the choice is always yours! You can be strengthened, and your resolve restored. You can soar with a newfound freedom, and meet new and stimulating opportunities in which to train, to learn, and to grow.

Affirmation: I AM choosing to continue my holistic journey of Rhythmic Training. I AM filled with the possibilities for a better me. I ask to make my choices carefully with the help of Spirit.

DAY FIVE

Exercise	Sets	Reps	Percentage	Rest	Comments
Warm-up and Stretching					
Back Squat	3	5	85%1RM	4 minutes	
Romanian DL	3	5	"		
Inline Lunge	3	5	"		
Bench Press	3	5	"		
Dips	3	5			
Side Bend Abs	3	30		20-30 seconds	

Friday

Prudent Strength

- Congratulations, you are one Shade closer. The Rhythmic Training Dance, though intense, is exhilarating, with sexy physique changes, beautiful Shades, and prudent functional health along the way. It builds your lungs and legs, as well as your mind and metabolism. You may have considered withdrawing when the sessions seemed to stretch endlessly before you.
- As the days wore on, however, you caught glimpses of your goal and decided that each Shade was bringing you closer.

Affirmation: I AM learning the rewards of strength, perseverance, faith, and love, for the joy and the work of attaining my health goals. I will weather this training process designed to assist in restoring and maintaining my healthy physique.

DAY SIX

Exercise	**Sets**	**Reps**	**Percentage**	**Rest**	**Comments**
Warm-up and Stretching					
Hang Clean	3	5	85%1RM	4 minutes	
Push Press	3	5	"		
Standing Low Row	3	5	"		
Neutral Grip Pull ups	3	5			

Hand Planks	3	45 seconds hold			

Saturday OFF
Light Transitions

- You have enjoyed the challenge and inherent comfort of the easy training times, when you were feeling no discomfort (DOMS). However, its purpose has been served. You are now prepared to transition into a stronger Shade.

Affirmation: I AM changing right now, allowing my system to transition. This time of transition invites progressing to another level of fine-tuning my body and tickling my soul. I make application to let this transition affect my courage and strength in fulfilling the possibilities of the coming Shade.

DAY SEVEN

REST Abdominals	**COMMENTS**

MAXIMUM STRENGTH SHADE

Green symbolizes Nature, abundance, and renewal. Throughout this Shade, in order to abundantly perpetuate, retain, and regain your youthful contours, we will bring you to the edges of your character and strength. Be aware of all plants and trees. Strategically, use them as reminders to breathe deeply and completely, and thank them for their ***energy***.

WEEK FOURTEEN

Sunday

The Longevity of Ecstasy

- Dancing through the Shades of rhythmic training is likened to a loving, intimate relationship—both ask you to expose your hidden self, to bare your soul, and deepens your awareness of pain and ecstasy. Erroneously it is thought that love as well as training only brings delight. Appreciatively, both are portals for promoting better living.

Affirmation: I AM exposing my spirit and my body to the training edges of pain and ecstasy, knowing that it increases the quality of my longevity. I have a quiet, expectant heart and mind—open to the heightened and deepened affair accompanying the next Shade.

DAY ONE

Exercise	Sets	Reps	Percentage	Rest	Comments
Warm-up and Stretching with Foam rolling					
Abdominals: Ab Wheel	1	15			
2-3 miles Out-door cardiovascular activity					

Monday

Preserving Your Majesty

- You are building up an endowment in disposition, mobility, and *self-efficacy* that will give you more balance, lean tissue, and personal power as you add years. Training is your body's opportunity to play. Thus, be sure your attitude is positive as it influences your mind, body, and soul.

Affirmation: I AM keeping my mind, body, and soul in condition consistently that the best may come to me. I desire to awaken and maintain a positive attitude for developing and preserving my body's majesty.

DAY TWO

Exercise	Sets	Reps	Percentage	Rest	Comments
Warm-up and Stretching					
Front Squat	3	3	70%1RM	3-5 minutes	

Romanian DL	3	3	"		
Step Ups	3	3	"		
DB Incline Bench Press	3	3	"		
Decline Abs.	2	15		20-30 seconds	

Tuesday
Confidence

- You are gaining strength: first it required a commitment, a decision. Next, it required training, and then persistent patience. Your strength to withstand stress, maintain ***energy***, and use the power of your breath is all increasing. The more you practice training, the more in touch with your body you are and that is where your true strength resides.

Affirmation: I AM fully attuned to the strength in complete acceptance of health and self-love, right here, right now. I will keep an open mind, train, and continue living from a place of confidence and strength.

DAY THREE

Exercise	**Sets**	**Reps**	**Percentage**	**Rest**	**Comments**
Warm-up and Stretching					
Clean	3	3	75%1RM	3-5 minutes	
Push Press	3	3	"		
Pull-ups	3	3			

Planks	2	20-30 seconds hold			

Wednesday

Energy

- Learning to train with both your physical and spiritual eyes open, you can be infused with a priceless ***energy*** surge.
- As your consciousness moves into a state of ***energy*** bliss, you will be lifted to new heights and weights of serene lifting confidence, and you will view training from a different perspective.

Affirmation: My heart is more joyful and free, my steps more light because I AM rhythmically training with a planned purpose and generating more ***energy***. I aspire to radiate a feeling of contentment within myself.

DAY FOUR

Exercise	Sets	Reps	Percentage	Rest	Comments
Warm-up and Stretching					
Abs. Circuit with Hips and Knees flexed to 90º:	2	40		20 seconds	
Elbow to Opposite Knee Crunches	1	30			

Bent-Knee Sit-up					
Cardio Interval Session 45 minutes**					

**Sessions can consist of bike, stepper, elliptical, rowing, swimming, walking, stationary bike, treadmill, or any other cardiovascular activity.

Interval Treadmill example: After a five minute warm-up, move treadmill to 15% grade and adjust the speed to a level where you're walking @ a VERY brisk pace. Walk for 15 seconds then step on side rails for 30 seconds. Repeat for 20 minutes, then finish with 10-15 minutes of steady-state walking (0-3% grade @ 3.0-3.5 KPH/MPH). If you decide to increase the work time, try to keep the rest ration at exactly twice the time you spend working.

Thursday
Self Mastery

- Your body is thriving and flourishing toward your desired goals. Rhythmically training and holistic dieting from the start is eliciting strength and preventing the development of negative health outcomes.

Affirmation: I AM fear-free, patient, focused, and committed to my health. I propose to dance steadily and master my quality of life.

DAY FIVE

Exercise	Sets	Reps	Percentage	Rest	Comments
Warm-up and Stretching					
Back Squat	3	3	75%1RM	3-5 minutes	
Romanian DL	3	3	"		
Front Lunge	3	3	"		
DB Bench Press	3	3	"		
Decline Abs.	2	15		20-30 seconds	

Friday
Perseverance

➢ Your diligence is necessary if you are to attain and maintain your health milestones. Epictetus said, "Any habit and faculty is preserved and increased by its corresponding action." One of the most important aspects of the Training Dance is to dance perseveringly.

Affirmation: I AM co-operating to find more lasting strength and mobility. I pray to acknowledge my training time and actions as gifts.

DAY SIX

Exercise	Sets	Reps	Percentage	Rest	Comments
Warm-up and Stretching					
Clean Shrugs	3	3	70%1RM	4-5 minutes	
Push Press	3	3	"		
Neutral Pull-up	3	3			
Planks	2	20-30 seconds hold			

Saturday OFF
Processing Change

- The process of cultivating change is seldom done with ease. Yet you can see many changes when you contemplate the time before you began this Rhythmic Training Dance.

Affirmation: I AM cultivating change by reflecting on the distance traveled in my thinking, dieting, and training, so that I will be unable to take these changes for granted. I desire to see that I AM fit and more functional as a result of carefully training my contours forward. Today!

DAY SEVEN

REST	**COMMENTS**
Abdominals	

WEEK FIFTEEN

Sunday

Sacred Voyage

- Every session and every prayer begins within your mind and heart. This is your converging place with Spirit. To assure that your house of power and prayer is beautiful and sacred, you examine your thoughts, your diet, and your emotions.
- As you stroll through your spiritual house, you release all negative or restricting thoughts and emotions. Likewise, as you stroll through your physical house, allow your breathing to release all tension and stress—from the tips of your toes to the crown of your head—which may lead to undesirable feedings.
- Now free from those things that deprive your happiness, joy, and freedom of movement, you welcome positive healing thoughts of love and trust. You reside in this physical house for Spirit. It is up to you to create the healthiest house

possible.

Affirmation: I AM willing to do all that it takes to continue on my training journey, and it takes plenty, and I know I have all that it takes. I desire that in these quiet moments of introspection, my mind and my body become a sacred sanctuary.

DAY ONE

Exercise	Sets	Reps	Percentage	Rest	Comments
Warm-up and Stretching with Foam rolling					
Abdominals: Ab Wheel	1	20			
2-3 miles Out-door cardiovascular activity					

Monday
Restoration

- Over time, showing an indifference to strength training shows up as immobility and postural imbalances later. Before completing the Shades you will know time is sublime; wherein, you desire to own no body but your own.

Affirmation: I AM reducing stress, improving circulation, and heightening my spirit. I ask to continue practicing preventative and restorative actions. Period!

DAY TWO

Exercise	Sets	Reps	Percentage	Rest	Comments
Warm-up and Stretching					
Front Squat	3	3	75%	3-5 minutes	
Romanian DL	3	3	"		
Step Ups	3	3	"		
DB Incline Bench Press	3	3	"		
Decline Abs.	3	15		20-30 seconds	

Tuesday
Progression

➢ You will find that little by little you can let go of the old way of dieting—the one that barely worked—for holistic dieting that can and does work.

Affirmation: I AM opening myself to possibilities of change. I seek to follow the principle of progression. I no longer fight nor control. I simply trust Divine Love. I pray to empty myself to be full of awareness, strength, and love, and to face this training day with hope.

DAY THREE

Exercise	Sets	Reps	Percentage	Rest	Comments
Warm-up and Stretching					
Clean	3	3	80%1RM	3-5 minutes	
Push Press	3	3	"		
Pull-up	3	3			
Planks	3	20-30 seconds hold			

Wednesday

Natural Diversity

- By rhythmically training, you are providing occasions to stimulate, relax, and relieve fear and pain. Its very naturalness and flexibility make it possible to adapt and function in a manner unduplicated by any other modality.

Affirmation: I AM reinforcing my body's capacity to heal and naturally be healthy. I pray to fully embrace all these occasions to nourish, improve, and stimulate my body's natural diversity.

DAY FOUR

Exercise	Sets	Reps	Percentage	Rest	Comments
Warm-up and Stretching					
Abs. Circuit with Hips and Knees flexed to 90º:	2	40		20 seconds	
Elbow to Opposite Knee Crunches Bent-Knee Sit-up	1	30			
Cardio Interval Session 45 minutes**					

**Sessions will consist of bike, stepper, elliptical, rowing, swimming, walking, stationary bike, treadmill, or any other cardiovascular activity.

Interval Treadmill example: After a five minute warm-up, move treadmill to 15% grade and adjust the speed to a level where you're walking @ a VERY brisk pace. Walk for 15 seconds, then step on side rails for 30 seconds. Repeat for 20 minutes, then finish with 10-15 minutes of steady-state walking (0-3% grade @ 3.0-3.5 KPH/MPH). If you decide to increase the work time, try to keep the rest ration at exactly twice the time you spend working.

Thursday
Conquer Division

- Are you living in your entire body? Are you purposely distancing some parts?
- This Rhythmic Training Dance gives you the freedom to answer this honestly. As you move through the Shades, you are changed, and then you look with a new perspective on living fully in your body.

Affirmation: I AM continually refining my relationship to my body and to my food choices. I invite finer clarity and definition on how to continue experiencing and valuing my ever changing body.

DAY FIVE

Exercise	**Sets**	**Reps**	**Percentage**	**Rest**	**Comments**
Warm-up and Stretching					
Back Squat	3	3	80%1RM	3-5 minutes	
Romanian DL	3	3	"		
Front Lunge	3	3	"		
DB Bench Press	3	3	"		
Decline Abs.	3	15		20-30 seconds	

Friday

Filtering Contradiction

- You are daily choosing to train and move beyond the barriers in the way of your progress. Perchance there is some resistance. Yet hindsight assures you that you will move forward again, if you but have faith.

Affirmation: I AM reclaiming my holistic lifestyle, being whole, and loving myself through all barriers. I choose to have faith and fluidly train through any contradicting inner thoughts and feelings.

DAY SIX

Exercise	Sets	Reps	Percentage	Rest	Comments
Warm-up and Stretching					
Clean Shrugs	3	3	75%1RM	4-5 minutes	
Push Press	3	3	"		
Neutral Pull-up	3	3			
Planks	3	20-30 seconds hold			

Saturday OFF

Vigilance

- When you train with vigilance, power fills your being. It may come instantly and be quite obvious to you or it may come in its own time as a feeling of poised quiet and alignment.

Affirmation: I AM trusting that with every Shade of my holistic dieting expedition, I will feel and see the results when the time is right. I aspire to move gracefully through every Shade of my training.

DAY SEVEN

REST	**COMMENTS**
Abdominals	

WEEK SIXTEEN

Sunday

Process of Progression

- Whenever you train, do so with your whole heart. Permit yourself to become completely absorbed in your session because you have dedicated yourself to this dance. The progression is made simple, the training flows smoothly, and you receive so much more than you thought possible.
- When you train your Shades with careful movements, when you listen to your body with finely-tuned ears, when you see your progress with the eyes of love, you give 100 percent of

yourself, and your returns are augmented.

Affirmation: I AM open to the invitations awaiting me this session. I ask to flow smoothly into today's rhythm and progression.

DAY ONE

Exercise	Sets	Reps	Percentage	Rest	Comments
Warm-up and Stretchin g with Foam rolling					
Abdomin als: Ab Wheel	2	15		20-35 secon ds	
2-3 miles Out-door cardiova scular activity					

Monday
Dynamic Strength

- Daily you have certain responsibilities in your outer world. You have a responsibility to your family, your employer, your friends—people rely upon you.
- But there is more to life than meeting the needs of your outer world. There is an inner world in which you live. You have a responsibility to

develop this part of yourself.

➢ Take time to be with Spirit Force, to feel and develop spiritually as well as physically. These actions help you because both recharge your batteries. They give you peace and mobility enabling you to meet your outer responsibilities effectively.

Affirmation: I AM rhythmically training my body as a stronger base for my wisdom and my intellect to flourish, shine, and resound in my private and public life. I hope to focus on Spirit and trust my inner strength training to grow stronger in balancing my outer world's demands and responsibilities.

DAY TWO

Exercise	Sets	Reps	Percentage	Rest	Comments
Warm-up and Stretching and Stretching					
Front Squat	3	3	70%1RM	3-5 minutes	
Romanian DL	3	3	"		
Step Ups	3	3	"		
DB Incline Bench Press	3	3	"		
Decline Abs.	3	30		45 seconds	

Tuesday

Letting Go

- Does living in your body feel ***energetic*** and vibrant? Or do you feel like a forced tolerant keeper dragging your body around with you? Be honest.
- Your attitude and habits, whatever they may be, need never be unhealthy. Your Training Dance commitment and determination are initiating new patterns of healthy vibrant living—every hour, every snack, every week, every meal.

Affirmation: I AM parting with the old patterns in order to dance amidst the new positive ones. I tender to surrender and gently choose better healthier attitudes and actions.

DAY THREE

Exercise	**Sets**	**Reps**	**Percentage**	**Rest**	**Comments**
Warm-up and Stretching and Stretching					
Back Squat	3	3	70%1RM	3-5 minutes	
Romanian DL	3	3	75%1RM		
Step Ups	3	3	75%1RM		
DB Incline Bench Press	3	3	70%1RM		
Decline	2	15		20-30	

Abs.				seconds	

Wednesday
Diligence

➢ The Rhythmic Training Dance composes your mind as well as your body to draw out and invigorate your physical powers. Your body is unlike cars where you use them and immediately they begin to lose their value and shape accordingly. Bodies are the opposite: with diligent usage, it is in much better shape.

Affirmation: I AM directly rekindling and deepening the power and the condition of my mind, my body, and my soul. I ask to honor and diligently maintain the value of health throughout my day today.

DAY FOUR

Exercise	**Sets**	**Reps**	**Percentage**	**Rest**	**Comments**
Warm-up and Stretching					
Abs. Circuit with Hips and Knees flexed to 90°: Elbow to Opposite Knee Crunches Bent-	2 1	40 30		20 seconds	

Knee Sit-up					
Cardio Interval Session 45 minutes**					

**Sessions will consist of bike, stepper, elliptical, rowing, swimming, walking, stationary bike, treadmill, or any other cardiovascular activity.

Interval Treadmill example: After a five minute warm-up, move treadmill to 15% grade and adjust the speed to a level where you're walking @ a VERY brisk pace. Walk for 15 seconds, then step on side rails for 30 seconds. Repeat for 20 minutes, then finish with 10-15 minutes of steady-state walking (0-3% grade @ 3.0-3.5 KPH/MPH). If you decide to increase the work time, try to keep the rest ration at exactly twice the time you spend working.

Thursday
Celebrating You

- Your strength of mind, body, and soul are increasing. Just as you are learning the truth—you are totally responsible for governing and guiding your overall health.

Affirmation: I AM equipped to go to any length to improve my health. I propose to celebrate taking full responsibility for my *self-efficacy* and my health, choosing positive thoughts, nutrition-dense foods, training, and becoming my best self.

DAY FIVE

Exercise	Sets	Reps	Percentage	Rest	Comments
Warm-up and Stretching					
Clean	3	3	80%1RM	3-5 minutes	
Push Press	3	3	85%1RM		
Pull-up	3	3			
Planks	3	45 seconds hold			

Friday

The Ultimate Return

- Your living the Training Dance can work to effectively *recover, rejuvenate, return* muscle and joint function and ultimately improve health, increase spinal integrity, and reduce injury risk.

Affirmation: I AM managing my health and promoting the quality of my well-being. I pray to live the truth that my health is my wealth.

DAY SIX

Exercise	Sets	Reps	Percentage	Rest	Comments
Warm-up and Stretchin g					
Rack Clean	3	3	80%1RM	5 minute s	

Push Press	3	3	85%1RM		
Neutral Pull-up	3	3			
Planks	3	45 seconds hold			

Saturday OFF

The Wise Gift

- Your body is designed to move—that is the gift of its Designer. As you continue to discover, develop, and train you can discover seeds, plant them, nourish, and cultivate them; then harvest their fruits.
- Your maintenance of your God-given gift is like the planting of a seed. When you move this gift correctly, in a way that stimulates growth, you are supporting the seed to develop and increase. You reap the harvest of your gift by remaining mobile into your latter years.
- If you neglect to move and train your God-given gift, it atrophies and causes fruitless pain. The gift becomes de-conditioned and imbalanced. You stop growing and your well-designed system reaps less joy and delight.

Affirmation: I AM taking time to explore my mind, heart, and body. I AM training, maintaining, and developing more fully my own unique gift. I pray that with each Shade I take, I open a way to maintain myself, to learn about myself, and to be my higher self.

DAY SEVEN

REST	**COMMENTS**
Abdominals	

WEEK SEVENTEEN

Sunday

Beauty Building

- Your limits to attaining your health milestones are your fears and doubts. You are a spiritual being. Capable of astounding accomplishments, in possession of a body capable of moving in almost every imaginable direction. Because Truth is with you, be strong, confident, and courageous in living these Rhythmic Training Dance actions.

Affirmation: I AM gaining a new sense of what holistic living is all about. I ask to express my beauty and harmony openly, honestly, and firmly through living holistically and training.

DAY ONE

Exercise	Sets	Reps	Percentage	Rest	Comments
Warm-up and Stretching					

with Foam rolling					
Abdominals: Ab Wheel	2	15		20-25 seconds	
2-3 miles Out-door cardiovascular activity					

Monday
Maintenance

- Physical harmony and balance is pain with a purpose. Once you reach your goal, the work of stretching, hydrating, feeding, and guarding against atrophy begins. Producing and maintaining results is a lot of work.
- Your spiritual maintenance can be challenged by the state of the world. You can be calm in the midst of any storm by enduring on this voyage and respond to your fears with confidence.

Affirmation: I AM acquiring the discipline necessary to train and provide the best for my mind, body, and soul. I pray to appreciate that the harvest of training eminently overshadows any fear and pain.

DAY TWO

Exercise	Sets	Reps	Percentage	Rest	Comments
Warm-up and Stretching and Stretching					
Front Squat	3	3	80%1RM	3-5 minutes	
Romanian DL	3	3	"		
Step Ups	3	3	"		
DB Incline Bench Press	3	3	"		
Decline Abs.	3	30		20-30 seconds	

Tuesday

Buoyancy

- Your bones float in soft tissue. The Rhythmic Training Dance supports your body in maintaining the buoyancy of your joints and the integrity of your bones. To prevent long-term chronic postural impediments, you desire an even balanced tone across your muscles, so that your bones will stay lightly floating in their place.

Affirmation: I AM building my muscles to achieve and maintain the kind of balance that leads to ease, harmony, and lack of pain. I desire to provide the best support for the integrity and buoyancy of my posture.

DAY THREE

Exercise	Sets	Reps	Percentage	Rest	Comments
Warm-up and Stretching					
Clean	3	3	85%1RM	3-5 min utes	
Push Press	3	3	"		
Pull-up	3	3			
Planks	2	45 secon ds hold			

Wednesday
Trust

- You are learning to continue the training Shades with confidence, trusting that the ***energy*** and power you require will be given you.
- Congratulate yourself wherever you are today and celebrate your rising to the Training Dance challenge.

Affirmation: I AM changing and moving forward confidently. I ask for tranquility as I persist on this voyage of change and growing healthier.

DAY FOUR

Exercise	Sets	Reps	Percentage	Rest	Comments
Warm-up and Stretching					
Abs. Circuit with Hips and Knees flexed to 90º: Elbow to Opposite Knee Crunches Bent-Knee Sit-up	2 1	40 30		20 seconds	
Cardio Interval Session 45 minutes**					

**Sessions will consist of bike, stepper, elliptical, rowing, swimming, walking, stationary bike, treadmill, or any other cardiovascular activity.

Interval Treadmill example: After a five minute warm-up, move treadmill to 15% grade and adjust the speed to a level where you're walking @ a VERY brisk pace. Walk for 15 seconds, then step on side rails for 30 seconds. Repeat for 20 minutes, then finish with 10-15 minutes of steady-state walking (0-3% grade @ 3.0-3.5 KPH/MPH). If you decide to increase the work time, try to keep the rest ration at exactly twice the time you spend working.

Thursday
Faith

- Each day of the Training Dance brings you a newer you. In each breathtaking new moment, Spirit fills your mind with wisdom, your body with vitality, and your soul with tranquility.
- Breath is constant, and even when you make mistakes or poor choices, you are gently led back into the positive course of action. Therefore, stay centered and consistent with your training.

Affirmation: With each breath I take I know as I pursue my training, I AM guided and strengthened by Spirit Force. I pray to be upheld wherever I AM by an awareness of Spirit and the buoyancy of my faith whenever I need more strength.

DAY FIVE

Exercise	Sets	Reps	Percentage	Rest	Comments
Warm-up and Stretching					
Back Squat	3	3	85%1RM	3-5 minutes	
Romanian DL	3	3	"		
Front Lunge	3	3	"		
DB Bench Press	3	3	"		

Decline Abs.	3	30		30-45 seconds	

Friday
Mysterious Byproduct

- The Rhythmic Training Dance entices you to progress, discover, and thoroughly reflect. You deliberately challenge, listen, and most importantly, love and accept the physique you are expressing.

Affirmation: I AM attentively dancing and fully living as an additional byproduct. I pose to continue training and discovering that my diet actions and fear-free attitudes show the love I have for my health.

DAY SIX

Exercise	Sets	Reps	Percentage	Rest	Comments
Warm-up and Stretching					
Clean Shrugs	3	3	80%1RM	4-5 minutes	
Push Press	3	3	"		
Neutral Pull-up	3	3			
Side Planks	3	30-45 seconds hold			

Saturday OFF
Smile

- No training or effort is superfluous to your

development. You can reflect on yesterdays and smile because you showed up. You can look with anticipation at the Shades ahead—gifts—all of them. All sessions can be trusted to release your worries, freeing you to progress and go forth with an assurance that guides all training days.

Affirmation: I AM feeling and looking beautiful for the training done. I aspire to be more understanding and soothing with myself by smiling more often.

DAY SEVEN

REST	**COMMENTS**
Abdominals	

RECOVERY TRANSITION SHADE

Purple is symbolic of dignity, power, and royalty. Therefore it is an excellent choice for deep meditation. Throughout this Shade, use it to gain clearer insight and wisdom on your path thus far. Meditate on its power as you still your mind and promote your spirituality and strength. Some ***energy*** rich purple foods: blue grapes, broccoli, and eggplants.

<u>**WEEK EIGHTEEN**</u>

Sunday

Following the Flow

- Every detail of your holistic dieting and training is guiding you to accomplish your goal. A most beautiful transformation is taking place. If your results seem to be developing slower than your ego desires, cease being disheartened, be grateful you have initiated and are continuing the dance.

Affirmation: I AM following the flow of training, trusting that the results begin internally first. I will diet, train, and look neither back nor become disheartened, but be steady and move onward with courage.

DAY ONE

Exercise	Sets	Reps	Percentage	Rest	Comments
Continue with breathing, fine motor,					

and relaxation exercises and Abdominals of your choice.					

Monday

A.M. Visions

- Being enthusiastic and uncluttered each morning becomes a firm commitment only with diligence. Positive enthusiasms foster positive experiences. Trust that each Shade will be influenced by your spontaneous yet planned interaction with all the moments of each training day.

Affirmation: I AM enthusiastic about the new level of handling my mind, body and soul with care, awaiting me! I anticipate the best today, and know I will be enriched with the strength to train forward.

DAY TWO

Exercise	Sets	Reps	Percentage	Rest	Comments
Continue with breathing, fine motor, and relaxation exercises and Abdominals of your					

choice.					

Tuesday

Serene Surrenders

- The Rhythmic Training Dance renders you thoughtfully sexy, deliciously vulnerable, and functionally strong. It allows you to deliberately take time to survey and convey the beauty and strength in serene surrenders to increased external resistance. In this mysterious fashion, it fully commands attaining spiritual and physical harmony.

Affirmation: I AM serenely surrendering to the fullness of dancing through the next Shade. I will celebrate the harmonious outcome of all my dieting and training choices past, present, and future.

DAY THREE

Exercise	Sets	Reps	Percentage	Rest	Comments
Continue with breathing, fine motor, and relaxation exercises and Abdominals of your choice. **2-3 miles Outdoor cardiovascular activity**					

Wednesday

A Thankful Sentinel

➢ Your body has an amazing ability to grow, move, and heal. Therefore, throughout this day, thank Spirit-Force for your mind, body, and soul. And an opportunity to diet, train, and discover how to optimally maintain all of these.

Affirmation: I AM grateful for a structured way to guard my health. I choose to be grateful and thankful for this new start.

DAY FOUR

Exercise	**Sets**	**Reps**	**Percentage**	**Rest**	**Comments**
Continue with breathing, fine motor, and relaxation exercises and Abdominals of your choice.					

Thursday

Gradual Growth

➢ The more you develop your spirit and body, the more intense and challenging your path seems to become. Regardless of how intense the training becomes, regardless of how challenging, how inconvenient the sessions or the situations, these are rewards. That reward lies in your adding years with fear-free thinking, mobility, and strength.

Affirmation: I AM continuing onward into the natural pattern of increased intensity and growth. I will seek to incorporate, in no uncertain terms, the unfolding challenges in endurance and progression.

DAY FIVE

Exercise	Sets	Reps	Percentage	Rest	Comments
Warm-up and Stretching					
Deadlifts		10	80%1RM		
Bent Over Row		10	"		
Hang Cleans		10	"		
Push Press		10	"		
Front Squat		10	"	2-3 minutes then repeat once for a total of 2 Sets.	
Crunches	1	25			

Friday

Whose Accountability?

- Often times, you may feel a reverberating discontent for holistic dieting and training, or think of excuses for stopping. In spite of that, you know you get some lift after every lift. And you know in some indescribable way your life has been made richer, just for showing up.

Affirmation: I AM showing up for the next Shade of training because that is the only way I can achieve my long-range goal. I will carry on with confidence. At the end of each Shade, I feel a special sense of accomplishment, a richness that is inexplicable and that makes me want more.

DAY SIX

Exercise	Sets	Reps	Percentage	Rest	Comments
Continue with breathing, fine motor, and relaxation exercises and Abdominals of your choice.					

Saturday OFF

Beneath the Exterior

- Your efforts invested in living the Training Dance provide some much-needed guidance in managing your stress. The demands will afford you the physique harmony you seek.

Affirmation: I AM living more in harmony with my inner-self and my outer world. I pray to gradually become more stress-free and guided.

DAY SEVEN

REST	COMMENTS
Abdominals	

WEEK NINETEEN

Sunday

Envisioning the Whole

- Rest, contemplation, and quiet enjoyment of selected foods, opens the portal of interconnecting beauty and preparation of your mind, your body, and your spirit during transitioning.

Affirmation: I AM a whole and complete person, who deserves to ingest whole foods and complete proteins. I ask to service my body with a spirit of love, harmony, and humility in my dietary and training practices.

DAY ONE

Exercise	Sets	Reps	Percentage	Rest	Comments

Continue with breathing, fine motor, and relaxation exercises and Abdominals of your choice.					

Monday
Gratitude

- Remember that the only place where strength, serenity, and success come before training is in the dictionary.

Affirmation: I AM discharging the total weight of my inner resources behind my endeavors. I desire to feel enduring gratitude for the opportunity of physical, mental, and spiritual development Rhythmic Training has brought me.

DAY TWO

Exercise	**Sets**	**Reps**	**Percentage**	**Rest**	**Comments**
Warm-up and Stretching					
Back Squat	1	5	70%1RM	2-3 minu tes	
	1	5	80%1RM		
Bench Press	1	5	70%1RM		

	1	5	80%1RM		
Deadlifts	1	5	70%1RM		
	1	5	80%1RM		
Leg Raises	1	20			
Back Extension s	1	20			

Tuesday

Assessing Forward

- How curious to think back to the months when you were just beginning the Training Dance routine.
- Your decision and diligence has generated you in unexpected ways. Well done, forget what lies behind. Squat, lift, press, and holistically feed forward.

Affirmation: I will continue to support my mind, my body, and my spirit since health and harmony are no longer a theory.

DAY THREE

Exercise	Sets	Reps	Percentage	Rest	Comments
Continue with breathing, fine motor, and relaxation exercises and Abdominals of your					

choice.					

Wednesday

A Challenge of Transitions

- You own a new physique skillfully built on the foundation of sound dieting and training woven together.
- Distractions come in all shapes and sizes. You are so close, so remember the focus and enthusiasm which are behind while reaching forward to the Shade ahead.

Affirmation: I AM something new and I AM willing to explore new depths.

DAY FOUR

Exercise	**Sets**	**Reps**	**Percentage**	**Rest**	**Comments**
Warm-up and Stretching					
Abdominals: Ab Wheel	3	10		20 seconds	
Cardio: 20-30 minutes Out-door cardiovascular activity			70-75% predicted maximum heart rate		

Thursday
Insight

- You must beware of the deceptive current of "leisurely" over-eating. Training can become tedious. You may get tired of focusing, pushing, pressing, curling, cardio, and then juicing, preparing and ingesting whole foods. But being fear-free and looking delicious, sexy, firm, and healthy is never passé or tedious!
- What a joy when you see the resultant process in the mirror. Remember that this resultant is guaranteed for a lifting lifetime.

Affirmation: I AM grateful to Spirit Force and I AM blessed by this opportunity for my own delicious maintenance and advancement.

DAY FIVE

Exercise	Sets	Reps	Percentage	Rest	Comments
Continue with breathing, fine motor, and relaxation exercises and Abdominals of your choice.					

Friday

More than Knowing

- Just having knowledge is subpar. The key to your success in health will be in wisely applying everything you have learnt. The Rhythmic Training Dance is a solution to wholeness, health, and stress free living. "Live in the solution."

Affirmation: I AM motivated by self-love! Therefore, I resolve to live, in actions and attitude, the wisdom that has come to me. I accept that ignorance can no longer be my excuse.

DAY SIX

Exercise	Sets	Reps	Percentage	Rest	Comments
Continue with breathing, fine motor, and relaxation exercises and Abdominals of your choice.					

Saturday OFF

New Dimensions

- A new Shade of sets and repetitions awaits you. You must decide you are ready, willing, and open to inspiringly train forward. Every Shade is designed for your betterment. Accept and respect your progression, you have earned it.

Affirmation: I AM rewarding myself by lovingly progressing to new dimensions of training specificity. I propose to cooperate and really follow the Shades.

DAY SEVEN

REST	**COMMENTS**
Abdominals	

MAXIMUM FAT LOSS SHADE

Carb Sundays: On your calendar, mark off every other Sunday. On these days you can ingest additional carbs. Not too many. Choose wisely and thoroughly enjoy them!

Protein Intake: In the course of a Maximum Fat Loss Shade, always increase your protein intake, because if the rate of protein breakdown exceeds the rate of protein synthesis, you will lose muscle mass. This increased protein helps to preserve your muscles with your decreased carbohydrate intake.

Yellow is closely akin to clarity, healing, and confidence. Pay attention to all the places you see yellow in the world. Is it pale yellow or bright yellow? You may desire to wear or carry something yellow as a pleasant tribute to your clarity in achieving the goal of this Shade: Gaining a steady rhythm of motion while maintaining overall muscular strength and balance through your body and soul, as you confidently diminish nonessential fear and fat.

<u>WEEK TWENTY</u>

Sunday

Purpose

- Rhythmic Training connects you to what is facile and natural. Beginning each Dance Shade can teach you to slow down and feel the splendor of moving in your body. You can find the glory of your power in the brief course of a session with the bliss of breath and gravity.

Affirmation: I AM training for a purpose—staying healthy for the long term. I propose that training will help my spiritual power to pattern my physical and mental power.

DAY ONE

Exercise	**Sets**	**Reps**	**Percentage**	**Rest**	**Comments**
Warm-up and Stretching					
Front Squat	2	10-12	67%1RM	60 seconds	
	3	8-10			
Superset: Back Squat Single-Leg DL	2 2	10-12 8-10	"	90 seconds	
Inline Lunge	3	8-10		60 seconds	
Hack Squat	3	15		90 seconds	
Superset Abs: Back raises Decline Twists	3 3	15 20		30 seconds	

Monday

The Checkup

- Think, "Why am I eating?"
- Ask Spirit Force to help you watch why and

what you are ingesting, that it may truly be a reflection of holistic dieting.

- If you are eating to quell some emotion, ask to find the space between your impulse and your ingesting, to let a calming breath flow through you before you ingest all meals today.

Affirmation: I AM taking my time to taste, savor, and enjoy my meals. I AM making healthier choices. I pray to begin and continue knowing why I AM ingesting.

DAY TWO

Exercise	**Sets**	**Reps**	**Percentage**	**Rest**	**Comments**
Warm-up and Stretching					
Bench Press	4	10-12	67%1RM	60 seconds	
Pull-up	4	10-12	50%1RM		
Superset: DB Decline Bench press Seated Low-row	4	10-12	67%1RM	90 seconds	
Superset: Incline Close-grip bench press Hammer curls	4	10	"	60 seconds	
Decline Abs.	4	15		20-25 seconds	

Cardio: Treadmill or Outdoor Hills for **30 minutes**			15% grade @ 3.0 mph Hills@ 70-75% predicted maximum heart rate		

Tuesday
Progress

- Your acceptance to live the Training Dance challenge is making you grow into a healthier person. Make each training session one of progress, steady progress.

Affirmation: I AM advancing with each session regardless of what happens or what my mind may say. I ask that I will never again make a mess of my physique through fear and voracious feedings.

DAY THREE

Exercise	**Sets**	**Reps**	**Percentage**	**Rest**	**Comments**
Warm-up and Stretching					
Foam Rolling					
Abdominals: Swiss ball Reverse Crunches to failure	5	10		25 seconds	
Cardio: Treadmill or			15% grade		

Outdoor Sprints			@ 3.0 mph Warm-up 5minutes then @ 6.0 mph 10 Intervals of 30 sec. Run 60 sec. Jog Cool-down 5 minutes		

Wednesday
Living Light

- The dictionary defines beauty as "qualities which give pleasure to the esthetic sense, as by line, form, texture, rhythmic motion, or by behavior and attitude." Through training and holistic dieting you naturally create the *self-efficacy* that reflects your light and your lines of definition.
- Holistic living is a habit and a habitation of the harmony and beauty that abides in Spirit.

Affirmation: I AM embracing my training and health as a perpetual "checks and balances" sheet of my mental, physical, and spiritual awareness. I pray that this day my natural beauty and spirit illuminates through my diet, training, and living.

DAY FOUR

Exercise	Sets	Reps	Percentage	Rest	Comments
Warm-up and Stretching					
Stiff-leg DL	4	10-12	67%1RM	60 seconds	
Superset: Wide-stance Back Squat Good Morning	4	12	"	90 seconds	
Side Lunge	3	8	"	60 seconds	
Leg curl	3	15	"	90 seconds	
Superset Abs: Toe touches Bicycles Side Planks		20 30 30 sec. hold each side			

Thursday

Energy

➢ You know that putting on fat is a storage mechanism of your body that was useful in primitive times and during famine. You now have access to foods of many tempting varieties, so discipline must apply somewhere.

➢ Your courage to follow the Rhythmic Training Dance is a key to unlocking and erecting your storehouse of ***energy***, strength, and confidence.

Affirmation: I AM dancing to decrease fat permanently. Therefore, I AM decreasing my input of deficient food ***energy***. I ask to continue training and applying holistic dieting to change the contours of my confidence as well as my body.

DAY FIVE

Exercise	**Sets**	**Reps**	**Percentage**	**Rest**	**Comments**
Warm-up and Stretching					
Foam Rolling					
Decline Abs.	10	10		20-25 seconds	
Cardio: Treadmill or Outdoor Hills for **30 minutes**			15% grade @ 3.0 mph Hills@ 70-75% predicted maximum heart rate		

Friday

Love

➢ My heart sings with the music of loving

myself. My love brings with it meaningful responsibility. And I want always to be certain that I AM doing all that I can to grow in the healthiest manner possible.

➢ I prepare well-constructed balanced meals and use my ***energy*** sources wisely.

➢ I know that whatever I do out of this love is important and adds joy to my life, to the lives of my family, and others.

Affirmation: I AM reclaiming my right and responsibility for living healthier. I pray that self-love continues to motivate me in living the Training Dance.

DAY SIX

Exercise	**Sets**	**Reps**	**Percentage**	**Rest**	**Comments**
Warm-up and Stretching					
Seated DB Press	4	10	67%1RM	60 seconds	
Wide Pull-up	4	10	50%1RM	60 seconds	
Superset: Seated Lateral raise Rope Lat-pulldowns	4	10	"	90 seconds	
Superset: Overhead Cable Triceps extensions Cable curls	4	10	"	60 seconds	

Superset Abs: Standing DB Twists Side Bends	2	15		20 seconds	
Cardio: Elliptical for **30 minutes**			Level 4-6		

Saturday OFF

Beyond the Horizon

- Your path forward is as certain as your commitment to it. Your belief in the principles of the Training Dance and your faith that your body is transforming, even when you are confronted with major or minor adversities.
- Respectful attention to your health steers your wealth.

Affirmation: I AM wide awake and taking responsible diet actions for my mental, physical, and spiritual development. I ask to continue training and giving sincere attention and priority to attaining optimal health.

DAY SEVEN

REST	**COMMENTS**
Abdominals	

WEEK TWENTY-ONE

Sunday

Perseverance

- You can persevere and preserve your holistic dieting through adverse conditions and circumstances by practicing Rhythmic Training and trusting the Spirit of Love.
- Instead of adding weight and gaining unnecessary fat, you gain a new perspective of self.

Affirmation: I AM preserving a nourishing relationship with Divine Love, holistic dieting, and training. I anticipate gaining conscious comfort in living healthier.

DAY ONE

Exercise	Sets	Reps	Percentage	Rest	Comments
Warm-up and Stretching and Stretching					
Front Squat	2	10-12	67%1RM	60 seconds	

	3	8-10			
Superset: Back Squat Single-Leg DL	2 2	10-12 8-10	"	90 seconds	
Inline Lunge	3	8-10		60 seconds	
Hack Squat	3	15		90 seconds	
Superset Abs: Back raises Decline Twists	3 3	15 20		30 seconds	

Monday

Tuning Your Instrument

- You must objectively sustain your willingness to train because your body is a magnificent instrument! With holistic dieting and training you appreciate its functional capacity. And being finely-tuned, your instrument will work more sharply and keenly due to hours of precision feeding and training.

Affirmation: By dieting and training, I AM practicing fine-tuning, fear-free thinking, mobility, flexibility, and functioning of my divine instrument. I pray that as a result of living this dance, I will add much joy and suppleness to the working and the playing time of my instrument.

DAY TWO

Exercise	Sets	Reps	Percentage	Rest	Comments
Warm-up and Stretching					
Bench Press	4	10-12	67%1RM	60 seconds	
Pull-up	4	10-12	50%1RM		
Superset: DB Decline Bench press Seated Low-row	4	10-12	67%1RM	90 seconds	
Superset: Incline Close-grip bench press Hammer curls	4	10	"	60 seconds	
Decline Abs.	4	15		20-25 seconds	
Cardio: Treadmill or Outdoor Hills for **30 minutes**			15% grade @ 3.0 mph Hills@ 70-75% predicted maximum heart rate		

Tuesday
Broader Understanding

- Your unique beauty has its source in a powerful and timeless ***energy***. In a spiritual sense, your mental and physical health is essential for the sunlight of your beauty to be in a position of delicious reflection.

Affirmation: I AM holistically dieting and training to strategically expose the light of my natural beauty. I pray to direct and reflect the ***energy*** of my highest self in the best feasible light.

DAY THREE

Exercise	Sets	Reps	Percentage	Rest	Comments
Warm-up and Stretching					
Foam Rolling					
Abdominals: Swiss ball Reverse Crunches to failure	5	10		25 seconds	
Cardio: Treadmill or Outdoor Sprints			15% grade @ 3.0 mph Warm-up 5minutes then @ 6.0 mph 10		

			Intervals of 30 sec. Run 60 sec. Jog Cool-down 5 minutes		

Wednesday

True Partnership

- Practicing holistic dieting and the Training Dance will emerge into a new, deeper dimension in your relationship with your physique.

Affirmation: I AM reevaluating what I think I know to have a deeper relationship with the kinds of mental, physical and spiritual foods I require. I propose to compose a more delicious organic life.

DAY FOUR

Exercise	**Sets**	**Reps**	**Percentage**	**Rest**	**Comments**
Warm-up and Stretching					
Stiff-leg DL	4	10-12	67%1RM	60 seconds	
Superset: Wide-stance Back Squat Good Morning	4	12	"	90 seconds	

Side Lunge	3	8		60 seconds	
Leg curl	3	15		90 seconds	
Superset Abs: Toe touches Bicycles Side Planks		20 30 30 sec. hold each side			

Thursday

Desire

➢ You possess a transforming power within and that Power can direct and guide you through your resolve to live healthier.

Affirmation: I AM witnessing the effect of my unwavering commitment to fear-free living, dieting, and training. I desire to feel the depth and the transformative power of my *self-efficacy*.

DAY FIVE

Exercise	Sets	Reps	Percentage	Rest	Comments
Warm-up and Stretching					
Foam Rolling					
Decline Abs.	10	10		20-25 seconds	
Cardio:					

Treadmill or Outdoor Hills for **30 minutes**			15% grade @ 3.0 mph Hills@ 70-75% predicted maximum heart rate		

Friday
Recycle?

- Your holistic dieting and consistent training adroitly rebuilds your body's life-giving properties and symmetry. Remember: All natural foods contain the proper amount of acid and alkalinity in them, which your body requires to maintain optimal health.

Affirmation: I AM dieting and fearlessly living more in harmony with Nature's laws. I pray to cease ingesting recycled foods and follow this training dance Shade.

DAY SIX

Exercise	**Sets**	**Reps**	**Percentage**	**Rest**	**Comments**
Warm-up and Stretching					
Seated DB Press	4	10	67%1RM	60 seconds	
Wide Pull-up	4	10	50%1RM	60 seconds	
Superset: Seated Lateral raise Rope Lat-	4	10	"	90 seconds	

pulldowns					
Superset: Overhead Cable Triceps extensions Cable curls	4	10	"	60 seconds	
Superset Abs: Standing DB Twists Side Bends	2	15		20 seconds	
Cardio: Elliptical for **30 minutes**			Level 4-6		

Saturday OFF

Choosing the Present

- Every affirmation, every session, and every food choice defines your success in attaining physique harmony and beauty.

Affirmation: I AM acknowledging the beauty in the process of developing and maintaining my health. I choose to direct my ***energies*** to being open and totally present for all the wonders in the world this day.

DAY SEVEN

REST	**COMMENTS**
Abdominals	

WEEK TWENTY-TWO

Sunday

The Magnificent Eleven

- Your body is infused with eleven magnificent systems. They assimilate, circulate, eliminate, protect, and heal to keep damage to a minimum. It is the foundation that permits your fear-free thinking, stability, and mobility for living your decisions, priorities, and goals. Thus, maintaining and improving its health provides the most trustworthy foundation to building a solid life.

Affirmation: I AM dieting and training to nourish and strengthen the bonds of my magnificent eleven. I endeavor to stimulate, build, and reinforce a better relationship with the foundation of my whole health.

DAY ONE

Exercise	Sets	Reps	Percentage	Rest	Comments
Warm-up and Stretching					
Front Squat	2	10-12	67%1RM	60 seconds	
	3	8-10			
Superset: Back Squat Single-Leg DL	2 2	10-12 8-10	"	90 seconds	
Inline Lunge	3	8-10		60 seconds	
Hack Squat	3	15		90 seconds	
Superset Abs: Back raises Decline Twists	3 3	15 20		30 seconds	

Monday

Best Advocate

- The additional benefit of holistic dieting and Rhythmic Training is that you truly see, hear, and understand how no one else can be a better health advocate for you, than you.

Affirmation: I AM practicing self-discipline and experiencing the uniqueness of being healthier and wholly me. I cherish the foundation and the actions gained and offered through training, supporting, and producing a stronger mind, body, and soul.

DAY TWO

Exercise	Sets	Reps	Percentage	Rest	Comments
Warm-up and Stretching					
Bench Press	4	10-12	67%1RM	60 seconds	
Pull-up	4	10-12	50%1RM		
Superset: DB Decline Bench press Seated Low-row	4	10-12	"	90 seconds	
Superset: Incline Close-grip Bench press Hammer curls	4	10	"	60 seconds	
Decline Abs.	4	15		20-25 seconds	
Cardio: Treadmill or Outdoor Hills for **30 minutes**			15% grade @ 3.0 mph Hills@ 70-75% predicted maximum heart rate		

Tuesday
Projecting Self Trust

- You can trust how exciting it is to be your own sexy, ***energetic*** self. The Rhythmic Training Dance is also a process of revealing the softness and the quiet ***energy*** of strength.

Affirmation: I AM open and receptive to projecting my special qualities, the way I alone can. I shall look into my heart and begin my training day with a quiet trusting prayer.

DAY THREE

Exercise	**Sets**	**Reps**	**Percentage**	**Rest**	**Comments**
Warm-up and Stretching					
Foam Rolling					
Abdominals: Swiss ball Reverse Crunches to failure	5	10		25 seconds	
Cardio: Treadmill or Outdoor Sprints			15% grade @ 3.0 mph Warm-up 5 minutes then @ 6.0 mph		

			10 Intervals of 30 sec. Run 60 sec. Jog Cool-down 5 minutes		

Wednesday

Waiting is an Action

- Softly and tenderly, yet intensely and progressively you are training, training, waiting, and watching for the body you desire. Regular, persistent sessions are drawing you closer. Be patient.

Affirmation: I AM patiently dieting to manifest the transformation I want. I choose to stay motivated and continue this Rhythmic Training Dance despite any uncertainty that may cloud my vision.

DAY FOUR

Exercise	**Sets**	**Reps**	**Percentage**	**Rest**	**Comments**
Warm-up and Stretching					
Stiff-leg DL	4	10-12	67%1RM	60 seconds	
Superset: Wide-stance	4	12	"		

Back Squats Good Morning				90 seconds	
Side Lunge	3	8	"	60 seconds	
Leg curl	3	15	"	90 seconds	
Superset Abs: Toe touches Bicycles Side Planks		20 30 30 sec. hold each side			

Thursday

Relaxed Satisfaction

- You can delight in every fear-free thinking, diet and training action today, as your thoughts and your feelings are fresh, never to be repeated. So welcome the fullness and the simple satisfaction of knowing you are doing all that you can, the best you can, every moment of this day.

Affirmation: I AM relaxed, calm, and conscious of the richness of living this moment fully. I will delight in the fullness of speaking well and walking tall, for today will never be repeated in exactly the same way.

DAY FIVE

Exercise	Sets	Reps	Percentage	Rest	Comments
Warm-up and Stretching					
Foam Rolling					
Decline Abs.	10	10		20-25 seconds	
Cardio: Treadmill or Outdoor Hills for **30 minutes**			15% grade @ 3.0 mph Hills@ 70-75% predicted maximum heart rate		

Friday

Variety Rules

- You are a unique individual and fall neatly into no specified category. For that reason, you must make dietary changes suitable to your own body and where you are at this point. This is ultimately your ***energy*** and health maintenance voyage.

Affirmation: I AM efficiently planning and mixing my diet to include the best sources of all the nutrients required to effectively nourish my body. I do know what whole food and beverage choices work best for expressing and maintaining my best structural and functional health.

DAY SIX

Exercise	**Sets**	**Reps**	**Percentage**	**Rest**	**Comments**
Warm-up and Stretching					
Seated DB Press	4	10	67%1RM	60 seconds	
Wide Pull-up	4	10	50%1RM	60 seconds	
Superset: Seated Lateral raise Rope Lat-pulldowns	4	10	"	90 seconds	
Superset: Overhead Cable Triceps extensions Cable curls	4	10	"	60 seconds	
Superset Abs: Standing DB Twists Side Bends	2	15		20 seconds	
Cardio: Elliptical for **30 minutes**			Level 4-6		

Saturday OFF

Loving Another

- Your Rhythmic Training can benefit and change you to live deeper points of love and *self-efficacy*. You can offer all the encouragement and validation it has afforded you by inspiring someone else to have a goal of living healthier.
-

Affirmation: I AM living the changes through my diligence and the powerful precepts of the Training Dance Shades. I will extend the impact of my *self-efficacy* by supporting another in taking responsibility for the wealth of their health.

DAY SEVEN

REST	**COMMENTS**
Abdominals	

WEEK TWENTY-THREE

Sunday

You

- Your body systems are never isolated, and lack the freedom to optimally function separately, but rather they co-ordinate their activities to generate a unique state of order. Thousands of reactions are going on simultaneously to constitute the perfectly organized symphony of ***you.***

- Practiced co-ordination through rhythmic training commands results for your whole system.

Affirmation: I AM basking in the wonderful and subtle internal regulation of my body's ***energy*** and radiance. I seek to embrace the rhythmic, silent power, and freedom of owning an optimally healthy body.

DAY ONE

Exercise	Sets	Reps	Percentage	Rest	Comments
Warm-up and Stretching					
Superset: Cable-crosses Wide-grip bench press	5 5	12-15 8-10	60%1RM	90 seconds	
Superset: Seated lateral raise Neutral DB press	5 5	12-15 8-10	55%1RM	"	
Superset: Lying DB Triceps Extension Close-grip bench press	5 5	12-15 8-10	"	"	
Ab Wheel	2	15		20-25	

				seconds	
Cardio: Treadmill or Outdoor Hills for **35 minutes**			12% grade @ 3.0 mph Hills @ 70-75% predicted maximum heart rate		

Monday

Renewed Efforts

- When you desire optimal health you train for it, you diet for it, you trust in the best, and you take actions to produce it.

Affirmation: I AM never too busy to continue my collaborative health efforts. I desire to do the small tasks of producing a healthy mind in a healthy body. .

DAY TWO

Exercise	**Sets**	**Reps**	**Percentage**	**Rest**	**Comments**
Warm-up and Stretching					
Superset: Leg Extension Back Squat	5	12-15 8-10	60%1RM	90 seconds	
Superset: Leg Curl Stiff-leg DL	5	12-15	"	90 second	

		8-10		s	
Superset: Seated Calf raise Standing Calf raise	5	12-15 8-10	"	90 seconds	
Abdominals. Landmines	1	15			
Light Cardio: Elliptical for **15 minutes**			Level 1		

Tuesday

Discipline + Focus + Work = Results

- Who you are is beautiful! You are capitalizing on the credence of self-discipline. Your learnt willingness and mindset has allowed you to express greater health. Continue to guard your focus as your mind, physique, and soul mature.

Affirmation: I AM standing on my fear-free commitment to train more and complain less each day. I can accomplish any goal through self-discipline, willingness to work, and guarding my focus.

DAY THREE

Exercise	Sets	Reps	Percentage	Rest	Comments
Warm-up and Stretching					
Superset: Low- Pulley Seated Row Rope to Chest	5	12-15	60%1RM	90 seconds	

Rows Seated Row Machine		8-10			
Superset: Wide-grip Preacher Curl Standing BB Curl	5	12- 15 8-10	55%1RM	90 seconds	
Superset: Bent-over lateral raise Low- Pulley Seated Row Rope to Face Rows	5	12- 15 8-10	“	90 seconds	
Abdominals. Inchworm		12- 15			
Cardio: Treadmill or Outdoor Hills for **35** **minutes**			12% grade @ 3.0 mph Hills@ 70-75% predicted maximum heart rate		

Wednesday
Homeostasis

➢ Medical science has no cure for stress and denies the impact and the influence of your emotional or mental state on your physical well-being. Yet, about 70 percent of our population has maladies which are stress-related. Therefore stress is the number one killer.

➢ Conversely, the stress and adaptations of your physique's natural ***energy*** flow can be used to alleviate some of the numerous ailments related to stress.

Affirmation: I AM consciously activating and directing my ***energies*** to heighten my focus and alleviate distress. I can selectively use my holistic feedings and rhythmic training to maintain homeostasis through all my interactions.

DAY FOUR

Exercise	**Sets**	**Reps**	**Percentage**	**Rest**	**Comments**
Warm-up and Stretching					
Abdominals:					
5 pound Plate Planks	3	5 each side		20 seconds	
Cardio: Treadmill or Outdoor Hills for **40 minutes**			12% grade @ 3.0 mph Hills@ 70-75% predicted maximum heart rate		

Thursday
Prudent Planning

- Learning to rhythmically train and maintain is facilitated, you have discovered, by introducing selected diet combinations—yet being sensible and planning with flexibility.

Affirmation: I AM planning my meals to save my health, because I know neglecting meals can leave me unsettled. I will continue practicing nourishing diet choices to stay in the rhythm of my own special health standard.

DAY FIVE

Exercise	Sets	Reps	Percentage	Rest	Comments
Warm-up and Stretching					
Superset: Incline DB Fly Low- Incline Bench DB Press	5	12-15 8-10	60%1RM	90 seconds	
Superset: DB Frontal Raise Military Press	5	12-15 8-10	55%1RM	90seconds	
Superset: Rope Triceps Extension Decline Close-grip bench press	5	12-15 8-10	"	90 seconds	

Superset Abdominals: Leg Raise Hip Raise	 1	 15 15			
Cardio: Treadmill or Outdoor Hills for **35 minutes**			12% grade @ 3.0 mph Hills @ 70-75% predicted maximum heart rate		

Friday

Connective Awareness

- You know that highly processed food has "additives." Your full decision to rhythmically train and increase your awareness of when, what, and why you feed with no conditions has simplified your fear-free living, weight management, and health goals.

Affirmation: I AM training simplistically and dieting holistically to maintain the majesty of my physique. I pray to remember that all "additives" in foods create needs which may prove deleterious to my optimal health decisions and goals.

DAY SIX

Exercise	Sets	Reps	Percentage	Rest	Comments
Warm-up and Stretching					
Superset: Straight-arms Pulldown Lat Pulldown	5	12-15 8-10	60%1RM	90 seconds	
Superset: Incline DB curl Hammer curl	5	12-15 8-10	"	90 seconds	
Superset: BB Shrugs Lying DB Lateral Raises	5	12-15 8-10 each arm	" Minimal weight	90 seconds	
Abdominals: Side Bends	1	20			
Cardio: Treadmill or Outdoor Hills for **35 minutes**			12% grade @ 3.0 mph Hills@ 70-75% predicted maximum heart rate		

Saturday OFF
Practice

- ➢ You know by now that optimal physical health requires work to maintain it. Rhythmically training with this conviction will make fear-free living and holistic dieting more productive as well as more attractive.

Affirmation: I AM prudently living the Training Dance. I ask to practice what I know with a relaxed, focused, and consistently positive attitude.

DAY SEVEN

REST	**COMMENTS**
Abdominals	

WEEK TWENTY-FOUR
Sunday
Living the Dream

- A part of the beauty of rhythmically training is remembering that physique salubrity is a process with shades, transitions, and progressions. It is validating your ability, increasing your confidence, and most importantly, creating a fear-free, leaner you.

Affirmation: I AM actively seeking the best in myself. I desire that the reality of training be more gratifying than the dream of training for perfection.

DAY ONE

Exercise	Sets	Reps	Percentage	Rest	Comments
Warm-up and Stretching					
Superset: Cable-crosses Wide-grip bench press	5 5	12-15 8-10	60%1RM	90 seconds	
Superset: Seated lateral raise Neutral DB press	5 5	12-15 8-10	55%1RM	"	
Superset: Lying DB Triceps Extension Close-grip bench press	5 5	12-15 8-10	"	"	
Ab Wheel	2	15		20-25 seconds	
Cardio: Treadmill or Outdoor Hills for **35 minutes**			12% grade @ 3.0 mph Hills @ 70-75% predicted maximum heart rate		

Monday

Perseverance

- Pathologies may be global, but does this make them healthful or natural. Today, it is your choice. Your senses are your means of communication. Consciously create vivid mental images to support your training efforts. Repeatedly hear, see, feel, touch, taste, and smell the positive aspects of dieting more naturally and fear-free living with radiant health and vigor.

Affirmation: I AM using my mind to motivate and magnify my powers of perseverance. I choose to live dis“ease” free and healthy.

DAY TWO

Exercise	**Sets**	**Reps**	**Percentage**	**Rest**	**Comments**
Warm-up and Stretching					
Superset: Leg Extension Back Squat	5	12-15 8-10	60%1RM	90 seconds	
Superset: Leg Curl Stiff-leg DL	5	12-15 8-10	“	90 seconds	
Superset: Seated Calf raise Standing Calf raise	5	12-15 8-10	“	90 seconds	
Abdominals					

Landmines	1	15			
Light Cardio: Elliptical for **15 minutes**			Level 1		

Tuesday

Ripened Responsibility

- The Rhythmic Training Dance opened an ***energy*** efficient portal that leads to being optimally healthy. You obliged to focus, concentrate, and specialize in what you can do best to improve and maintain your full physique harmony.

Affirmation: I AM doing my job of training and feeding responsibly. I desire to stay off that carousel of fear, poor dieting, inferior health, overfatness, and fruitless pain. I desire to have my best health and physique.

DAY THREE

Exercise	**Sets**	**Reps**	**Percentage**	**Rest**	**Comments**
Warm-up and Stretching					
Superset: Low- Pulley Seated Row Rope to Chest Rows Seated Row Machine	5	12-15 8-10	60%1RM	90 seconds	
Superset: Wide-grip	5	12-15	55%1RM	90	

Preacher Curl Standing BB Curl		8-10		seco nds	
Superset: Bent-over lateral raise Low- Pulley Seated Row Rope to Face Rows	5	12-15 8-10	"	90 seco nds	
Abdominals Inchworm		12-15			
Cardio: Treadmill or Outdoor Hills for **35 minutes**			12% grade @ 3.0 mph Hills@ 70-75% predicted maximum heart rate		

Wednesday

Climbing Your Ladder

➢ You are dancing up the ladder of training, which reaches into optimal mental, physical, and spiritual health. By persistent holistic dieting—persistent, firm, and simple willingness to rhythmically train—you achieve the full physique harmony and beauty you seek.

Affirmation: I AM obtaining simple joy, health, and harmony by living holistically. I propose to persistently practice climbing the training dance ladder as a lifestyle with faith and confidence.

DAY FOUR

Exercise	**Sets**	**Reps**	**Percentage**	**Rest**	**Comments**
Warm-up and Stretching					
Abdominals:					
5 pound Plate Planks	3	5 each side	20 seconds		
Cardio: Treadmill or Outdoor Hills for **40 minutes**			12% grade @ 3.0 mph Hills @ 70-75% predicted maximum heart rate		

Thursday
High Yield Living

- The Rhythmic Training Dance formula enables you to duplicate the elements that make for years of healthy, dis"ease" free, harmonious, vigorous living.

Affirmation: I AM continuing to *recover, rejuvenate, return* as to my diet, training, and rest for a life-time. I desire to fearlessly dance, diet, rest and improve the care and attention of my physique to produce high yield vigorous living.

DAY FIVE

Exercise	Sets	Reps	Percentage	Rest	Comments
Warm-up and Stretching					
Superset: Incline DB Fly Low- Incline Bench DB Press	5	12-15 8-10	60%1RM	90 seconds	
Superset: DB Frontal Raise Military Press	5	12-15 8-10	55%1RM	90 seconds	
Superset: Rope Triceps Extension Decline Close-grip bench press	5	12-15 8-10	"	90 seconds	
Superset Abdominals: Leg Raise Hip Raise	1	15 15			
Cardio: Treadmill or Outdoor Hills for **35 minutes**			12% grade @ 3.0 mph Hills @ 70-75% predicted maximum heart rate		

Friday

The Organic Link

- Today, as you train pay attention and link up all your senses:

Hear your blood flowing to your working musculature,

See your joints moving your muscles,

Feel the heat byproduct from the work,

Touch your breath as it cleanses your blood, and

Taste the ***energy*** and smell the allure from the holistic diet you adhere to collaborating, enabling your soul to have a better human experience.

Affirmation: I AM employing all that charismatically makes me divinely human. I will remember that optimal health can be as organic as linking up all my senses.

DAY SIX

Exercise	Sets	Reps	Percentage	Rest	Comments
Warm-up and Stretching					
Superset: Straight-arms Pulldown LatPulldown	5	12-15 8-10	60%1RM	90 seconds	
Superset: Incline DB curl Hammer curl	5	12-15 8-10	"	90 seconds	
Superset: BB Shrugs Lying DB	5	12-15	" Minimal	90 seconds	

Lateral Raises		8-10 each arm	weight		
Abdominals: Side Bends	1	20			
Cardio: Treadmill or Outdoor Hills for **35 minutes**			12% grade @ 3.0 mph Hills@ 70-75% predicted maximum heart rate		

Saturday OFF

Satiety

➢ You can persevere with this facile natural method to keep your fear-free thinking, mobility, and postural balance on track and in good health without the aid of drugs, medicines, and "additives." You might be surprised at what you can do to naturally have a healthy, happy life full of vigor and peace.

Affirmation: I AM training to use and strengthen my mind, body, and soul for satiety and success. I choose to persevere with this simple natural elixir. I trust that my persevering attitude will help me find the successes I deserve.

DAY SEVEN

REST	**COMMENTS**
Abdominals	

WEEK TWENTY-FIVE

Sunday

Focus

- Commit to looking at your dieting objectively, paying attention to recurring patterns. Do this without blame, shame, or guilt.
- What triggers you going off your diet? Boredom? Fear? Fatigue?
- If it is fear, fear is just unfocused ***energy***. Training in a focused milestone-oriented manner, you can build your ***energy*** and experience less fatigue.

Affirmation: I AM focusing on myself in a positive, growth-oriented manner. I AM investing in getting back my ***energy*** by feeding my mind, my physique, and my soul holistically. I pray to have new-found confidence and declare myself whole, happy, and healthy.

DAY ONE

Exercise	Sets	Reps	Percentage	Rest	Comments
Warm-up and Stretching					
Superset: Cable-crosses Wide-grip bench press	5 5	12-15 8-10	60%1RM	90 seconds	
Superset: Seated lateral raise Neutral DB press	5 5	12-15 8-10	55%1RM	"	
Superset: Lying DB Triceps Extension Close-grip bench press	5 5	12-15 8-10	"	"	
Ab Wheel	2	15		20-25 seconds	
Cardio: Treadmill or Outdoor Hills for **35 minutes**			12% grade @ 3.0 mph Hills @ 70-75% predicted maximum heart rate		

Monday
Faith

- When your mind is full of faith and your physique buoyant, due to your natural strength and ***energy***, it is then when you subtly enjoy the refined ***energy*** currents magnified through holistic feedings and training.

Affirmation: I AM disposed to cease ingesting anything that diminishes, contravenes, or perverts the optimal expression of my mind, body, and soul. I aspire to embrace the deep ***energy*** released and absorbed by rhythmically training.

DAY TWO

Exercise	Sets	Reps	Percentage	Rest	Comments
Warm-up and Stretching					
Superset: Leg Extension Back Squat	5	12-15 8-10	60%1RM	90 seconds	
Superset: Leg Curl Stiff-leg DL	5	12-15 8-10	"	90 seconds	
Superset: Seated Calf raise Standing Calf raise	5	12-15 8-10	"	90 seconds	
Abdominals: Landmines	1	15			

Light Cardio: Elliptical for **15 minutes**			Level 1		

Tuesday
Beyond Infancy

- You must create your own health; it is likened unto giving birth to yourself. The positive pleasures and pains of training speak in your conscience as well as rousing the expression of your strong physique.

Affirmation: I AM using holistic dieting and Rhythmic Training as stepping stones to the birthing process of living a purposeful, fear-free, and healthy life. I will do all that I can to continue my training through both the positive pleasures and the pains expressed!

DAY THREE

Exercise	Sets	Reps	Percentage	Rest	Comments
Warm-up and Stretching					
Superset: Low- Pulley Seated Row Rope to Chest Rows Seated Row Machine	5	12-15 8-10	60%1RM	90 seconds	
Superset: Wide-grip Preacher Curl Standing BB Curl	5	12-15 8-10	55%1RM	90 seconds	

Superset: Bent-over lateral raise Low- Pulley Seated Row Rope to Face Rows	5	12-15 8-10	"	90 seconds	
Abdominals. Inchworm		12-15			
Cardio: Treadmill or Outdoor Hills for **35 minutes**			12% grade @ 3.0 mph Hills @ 70-75% predicted maximum heart rate		

Wednesday
Power

- You are learning, growing, and changing as you build the strength of your physique. As you grow in understanding that dieting and training provides the strength to prevent hard, brittle, and painful joints, you become aware of the gift strength can be. As you reflect upon your physical power, take time to honor the reality of your connection to a spiritual power that is as close as your breath and your thoughts.

Affirmation: I AM happier, healthier, and grateful for finding strength mentally, physically, and spiritually. I can reflect and honor the strength and connective power of my breath and my thoughts.

DAY FOUR

Exercise	Sets	Reps	Percentage	Rest	Comments
Warm-up and Stretching					
Abdominals:					
5 pound Plate Planks	3	5 each side	20 seconds		
Cardio: Treadmill or Outdoor Hills for **40 minutes**			12% grade @ 3.0 mph Hills @ 70-75% predicted maximum heart rate		

Thursday

Simple Design

- Your rhythmic training, a diet of simple, nourishing foods, and adequate daily water intake is a design for beautiful admiration of your mind, body, and soul.

Affirmation: I AM willing to go the distance of the Rhythmic Training Dance to achieve elevation in my strength, demeanor, and *self-efficacy*. I ask to open my mind, body, and soul to the admiration of the beauty and the simplicity surrounding being healthy.

DAY FIVE

Exercise	Sets	Reps	Percentage	Rest	Comments
Warm-up and Stretching					
Superset: Incline DB Fly Low- Incline Bench DB Press	5	12-15 8-10	60%1RM	90 seconds	
Superset: DB Frontal Raise Military Press	5	12-15 8-10	55%1RM	90seconds	
Superset: Rope Triceps Extension Decline Close-grip bench press	5	12-15 8-10	"	90 seconds	
Superset Abdominals: Leg Raise Hip Raise	1	15 15			
Cardio: Treadmill or Outdoor Hills for **35 minutes**			12% grade @ 3.0 mph Hills @ 70-75% predicted maximum heart rate		

Friday
Ageless Finesse

- The condition of your physique strongly impacts how you feel and think; and a sound mind makes healthier decisions about diet, attitudes, and engaging in training as a viable pathway for better living. Now and as you add years.

Affirmation: I AM training to challenge my cognition and my physique to ensure that I maintain power, mobility, and a strong sense of well-being. I ask for the courage to live the Training Dance as a systematic strategy for diminishing distress and adding years with finesse.

DAY SIX

Exercise	Sets	Reps	Percentage	Rest	Comments
Warm-up and Stretching					
Superset: Straight-arms Pulldown LatPulldown	5	12-15 8-10	60%1RM	90 seconds	
Superset: Incline DB curl Hammer curl	5	12-15 8-10	"	90 seconds	
Superset: BB Shrugs Lying DB Lateral Raises	5	12-15 8-10 each arm	" Minimal weight	90 seconds	
Abdominals: Side Bends	1	20			

Cardio: Treadmill or Outdoor Hills for **35 minutes**			12% grade @ 3.0 mph Hills @ 70-75% predicted maximum heart rate		

Saturday OFF

Breathing

- Your breath is ignited by the same force that kindles the breezes, the seas, and the storms. Breathing clears your nasal passages, moistens and purifies inhaled ambient air, increases your breath span, and purifies your respiratory system. It arouses the internal vigor of your physique.

Affirmation: I AM gently breathing and aligning my thoughts to the Truth about my overall health. I invite better health by training to vivify my breath and enrich the flow of my fear-free thinking and mobility.

DAY SEVEN

REST	**COMMENTS**
Abdominals	

WEEK TWENTY-SIX

Sunday

Learning Never Stops

- I AM learning that I deserve a holistic way of life. The Rhythmic Dance of training is a holistic way of living. I see the power of wholeness effecting others. Since I have made a space for rhythmic training in my life, may I reserve that space for a lifetime.

Affirmation: I AM weaving the fibers of a new physique. I AM building a new physique on the sound principles of training. I pray to always dance this training as a student and reflect and incorporate all I AM learning.

DAY ONE

Exercise	Sets	Reps	Percentage	Rest	Comments
Warm-up and Stretching					
Superset: Bench Press Kettlebell or DB Squat	4	12-15	55-60%1RM	15 seconds	
Superset: Bent-over BB Row Romanian DL	4	12-15	"	15 seconds	
Superset: Military Press Leg Press	4	12-15	"	15 seconds	

Abdominals: Hip Thrusts	1	15			
Cardio: Treadmill or Outdoor Hills for **35 minutes**			12% grade @ 3.0 mph Hills @ 70-75% predicted maximum heart rate		

Monday

In the Garden

- You are your garden, and your training consistency has extolled rewarding results. More and more the garden of your physique is blossoming, but your unremitting compliance to live holistically is on-going, so attend any weeds sprouting with more dancing on the Shades of training.

Affirmation: I AM taking time to admire my progress and the lushness of my flowering physique. I ask to truly appreciate the progress of my training with gratitude.

DAY TWO

Exercise	**Sets**	**Reps**	**Percentage**	**Rest**	**Comments**
Warm-up and Stretching and Stretching					
Abdominals: Ab Wheel	5	12-		25	

		15		seconds	
Cardio: Treadmill or Outdoor Sprints			15% grade @ 3.0 mph Warm-up 5 minutes then @ 6.0 mph 10 Intervals of 30 sec. Run 60 sec. Jog Cool-down 5 minutes		

Tuesday

Waistline Partnership

- Late at night, the snacks both liquid and solid, may invite you in and taste momentarily great. But think about how those extra inches, those extra pounds, add up. Your clothing becomes tighter in all the undesired places, and you ignore this. Across time, you purchase new clothing—clothing with expandable waists and/or are loose fitting. Cease being appalled, and continue improving the quality of your life.

Affirmation: I AM continuing to form a better partnership with fear-free living, food, and beverages. I pray to listen and purchase healthier snacks so that I may maintain my waist.

DAY THREE

Exercise	Sets	Reps	Percentage	Rest	Comments
Warm-up and Stretching					
Superset: Decline Bench Press 45º Lunge	4	12-15	55-60%1RM	15 seconds	
Wide-grip Pull-up Kettlebell or DB Stiff-leg DL	4	12-15	"	15 seconds	
Seated DB Press Front Squat	4	12-15	"	15 seconds	
BB Body Drag Curl Close-grip Bench press	4	12-15	"	15 seconds	
Abdominals: V-ups Hip Ups Alternate Toe Touches	3	15		20-25 seconds	
Cardio: Treadmill or Outdoor Hills for **35 minutes**			12% grade @ 3.0 mph Hills@ 70-75%		

			predicted maximum heart rate		

Wednesday
Broadcast, I AM

- The Training Dance process is akin to a symphony ensuring that mind, body, and soul play in harmony towards your chosen health milestones. It will develop and exercise your physique to be strong and available to move with quality as you age.
- What thoughts are you sending? Your secret to success revolves around your ability to push through your fears and train towards your desires.

Affirmation: I AM now blessing my physique to broadcast total acceptance and unconditional love. I aspire to send positive messages to begin to discover that love, strength, and understanding has to live within me.

DAY FOUR

Exercise	Sets	Reps	Percentage	Rest	Comments
Warm-up and Stretching					
Abdominals: Bent-Knee Sit-up Crunches	2 2	12-15 12-15		20- 25 seconds 25 30 seconds	

Cardio: Treadmill or Outdoor Sprints			15% grade @ 3.0 mph Warm-up 5 minutes then @ 6.0 mph 10 Intervals of 30 sec. Run 60 sec. Jog Cool-down 5 minutes		

Thursday
Continuance

- As you "diet" holistically, you are partaking in all that is nutritious, including delicious beverages, snacks, and meals.
- As you become increasingly aware of the adaptations of training and holistic dieting within your mind and your physique, your spirit is lifted to new spiritual heights and you are sated with delicious ***energy.***

Affirmation: I AM holistically living my commitment of ingesting more nutrition-rich substances. I pray that every cell of my physique is infused by my active choices of strengthening and rejuvenating my health.

DAY FIVE

Exercise	Sets	Reps	Percentage	Rest	Comments
Warm-up and Stretching					
Superset: Incline DB Bench Press Sissy Squat(Wide-open)	4	12-15	55-60%1RM	15 seconds	
Superset: Low-Pulley Seated Row Leg Curl	4	12-15	"	15 seconds	
Superset: Alternate DB Curl Bent-over Triceps Extension	4	12-15	"	15 seconds	
Abdominals: Standing Twists	1	15			
Cardio: Easy Elliptical **15 minutes**			Level 1		

Friday

Commitment

- The Training Dance taught you that as

training progresses, so does *self-efficacy*. You can decide and choose which goals to pursue and when. The activities of each Shade, the courage, the strength, and the flexibility to express capabilities which seemed beyond your grasp. Now, you can find joy in your physique from the inside as well as the outside.

➢ Training is freedom, and freedom is choosing how to train.

Affirmation: I AM keeping the fire of inner commitments alive through continuing to make these fear-free and vital choices. I AM choosing to make progress. I pray to have the willingness to adapt and overcome false ideas about my physique and trust that personal choices can be made today.

DAY SIX

Exercise	**Sets**	**Reps**	**Percentage**	**Rest**	**Comments**
Warm-up and Stretching					
Abdominals: Single-Leg Bridge **Superset:** Heel Touches Hip-Ups Legs Crossed	3 2	20 20		20-25 seconds 25-30 seconds	
Cardio: Treadmill or Outdoor Sprints			15% grade @ 3.0 mph Warm-up		

			5 minutes then @ 6.0 mph 10 Intervals of 30 sec. Run 60 sec. Jog Cool-down 5 minutes		

Saturday OFF
Friendship

- Do you trust your physique? Can it depend on you to relax, release and let go of fear, provide nutrition-dense foods, to keep it aligned and firm, and functioning optimally?
- If so, your physique has a great friend.

Affirmation: I AM sustaining my training endurance so that I may go on enjoying those secret treasures and pleasures asked with my mind, body, and soul. I pray to have a purer relationship with myself, for the attention I give is a priceless communion.

DAY SEVEN

REST	**COMMENTS**
Abdominals	

WEEK TWENTY-SEVEN

Sunday

Appropriate Application

- There exist scores of information on the detrimental effects of nutrition-deficiency, overeating, and stress. Information is useless unless it is applied. When you reliably train, nourish and cleanse your physique properly, and douse it with sunshine, water, fresh air, and adequate rest, it will rejuvenate and maintain your health.

Affirmation: I AM dissipating excess fear and feedings which burdens, stresses, and pollutes my physique. I know that I can, and I will, practically apply the knowledge imparted by the Rhythmic Training Dance.

DAY ONE

Exercise	Sets	Reps	Percentage	Rest	Comments
Warm-up and Stretching					
Superset: Bench Press Kettlebell or DB Squat	4	12-15	55-60%1RM	15 seconds	
Superset: Bent-over BB Row Romanian DL	4	12-15	"	15 seconds	
Superset: Military Press	4	12-15	"	15 seconds	

Leg Press					
Abdominals: Hip Thrusts	1	15			
Cardio: Treadmill or Outdoor Hills for **35 minutes**			12º Incline @ 3.0 mph Hills @ 70-75% predicted maximum heart rate		

Monday
Now What?

> ➢ What an incredible feeling full physique health is! What an awakening about the threads of thinking, dieting, and training as an expedition. What power your commitment to radiant health is.

Affirmation: I AM renewing my commitment to training because it allows me to live healthier, and through healthier living, I add years of renewed zest. I choose to refresh the power of living a fear-free, radiant, and organic health.

DAY TWO

Exercise	Sets	Reps	Percentage	Rest	Comments
Warm-up and Stretching					
Abdominals:					

Ab Wheel	5	12-15		25 seconds	
Cardio: Treadmill or Outdoor Sprints			15% grade @ 3.0 mph Warm-up 5 minutes then @ 6.0 mph 10 Intervals of 30 sec. Run 60 sec. Jog Cool-down 5 minutes		

Tuesday

Cool Flowing Eruptions

- You are guided to express your physique harmony and beauty—what needs to come forward and what needs to be released and let go of. Your desire for optimal mental, physical, and spiritual health is likened to a stream of cool, refreshing water reaching out to immerse you.

Affirmation: I AM fully available for the multisystem flowing of the training Shade eruptions. I wish to train on, flow on, and grow on.

DAY THREE

Exercise	Sets	Reps	Percentage	Rest	Comments
Warm-up and Stretching					
Superset: Decline Bench Press 45⁰ Lunge	4	12-15	55-60%1RM	15 seconds	
Wide-grip Pull-up Kettlebell or DB Stiff-leg DL	4	12-15	"	15 seconds	
Seated DB Press Front Squat	4	12-15	"	15 seconds	
BB Body Drag Curl Close-grip Bench press	4	12-15	"	15 seconds	
Abdominals: V-ups Hip Ups Alternate Toe Touches	3	15		20-25 seconds	
Cardio: Treadmill or Outdoor Hills for **35 minutes**			12% grade @ 3.0 mph Hills @ 70-75% predicted maximum heart rate		

Wednesday
Constructive Reflection

- You can reflect backwards only to say 'what a strangely delicious path Rhythmic Training has afforded me.' Keep progressing forward; you are filled with Divine power.

Affirmation: I AM producing fear-free power, harvesting ***energy***, and managing my strength. I propose to keep treading the training path holistically, patiently, and serenely.

DAY FOUR

Exercise	Sets	Reps	Percentage	Rest	Comments
Warm-up and Stretching					
Abdominals: Bent-Knee Sit-up Crunches	2 2	12-15 12-15		20-25 seconds 25-30 seconds	
Cardio: Treadmill or Outdoor Sprints			15% grade @ 3.0 mph Warm-up and Stretching 5 minutes then @ 6.0 mph		

			10 Intervals of 30 sec. Run 60 sec. Jog Cool-down 5 minutes		

Thursday

Abating Negative Reactions

- You can protect your mental acuity, physical mobility, and spiritual awareness if you continually live fear-free, ingest and digest holistic foods, and train. These are conducive to healthy assimilation, elimination, circulation, and aging gracefully.

Affirmation: I AM following the training dance Shades because my fear-free thinking, mobility, stability, and health will retreat by neglect. I pray to acknowledge the truth that the less I train the less healthy I shall be and continue progressing forward.

DAY FIVE

Exercise	Sets	Reps	Percentage	Rest	Comments
Warm-up and Stretching					
Superset: Incline DB	4	12-	55-	15	

Bench Press Sissy Squat(Wide-open)		15	60%1RM	seconds	
Superset: Low-Pulley Seated Row Leg Curl	4	12-15	"	15 seconds	
Superset: Alternate DB Curl Bent-over Triceps Extension	4	12-15	"	15 seconds	
Abdominals: Standing Twists	1	15			
Cardio: Easy Elliptical **15 minutes**			Level 1		

Friday
Breathing

- One breath at a time, you can practice the indescribable joys of fully being you. Rhythmic Training heightens your awareness of your true-self. Today, acquiesce and allow each breath to fully disclose the richness of wholly being ***you.***

Affirmation: I AM appreciating the habit of being my best now. I pray to live my life as a blessing. Dancing, dieting, and living from my light, one breath at a time.

DAY SIX

Exercise	Sets	Reps	Percentage	Rest	Comments
Warm-up and Stretching					
Abdominals: Single-Leg Bridge **Superset:** Heel Touches Hip-Ups Legs Crossed	 3 2	 20 20		 20-25 seconds 25-30 seconds	
Cardio: Treadmill or Outdoor Sprints			15% grade @ 3.0 mph Warm-up 5 minutes then @ 6.0 mph 10 Intervals of 30 sec. Run 60 sec. Jog Cool-down 5 minutes		

Saturday OFF
Appreciation

- I thank Spirit for this Shade of training. Positive pain gave me the capacity to progress. Going deep before going on made me appreciate more my physique. Dieting, which I regarded as a weakness, transformed now is my rhythmic training base.

Affirmation: I AM wearing the fibers of a new physique! I AM a glorious new me. I AM free—unconditionally. My heart is full and my soul is free. I AM healthy. I AM stress and fear free. I AM sexy just fully being me. I pray to re-surrender with total commitment into the training dance of my body, my mind, and my spirit.

DAY SEVEN

REST	**COMMENTS**
Abdominals	

TRANSITION SHADE

Red symbolizes the right to have passion, courage, and radiant health. It serves and emits a compelling, positive vibration. Moderately, "Do whatever turns you on!"

WEEK TWENTY-EIGHT
Sunday
DAY ONE

Starting Position: Stand in front of the mirror in the buff.

Action: Look at your entire physique. Relax.

Say, *"I AM embracing the flow of joy and balance through and with my new life* ***energy****!"*

How do you feel about your coccyx, your coccygeal gland, your anus, your urinary organs, your legs, your feet, and your nose?

Briefly write it down.

Exercise	Sets	Reps	Percentage	Rest	Comments
Warm-up and Stretching					
Superset: BenchPress Kettlebell or DB Squat	2	20	55-60%1RM	15 seconds	
Superset: Bent-over BB Row Romanian DL	2	20	"	15 seconds	

Superset: Military Press Leg Press	2	20	"	15 seconds	
Superset: Wide-grip Preacher curl E-Z CurlOverhead Triceps Extension	2	20	"	15 seconds	
Abdominals: Leg Raise	1	20			

Monday

DAY TWO

<u>Starting Position</u>: Stand in front of the mirror in the buff.

<u>Action</u>: Relax. Look at your entire physique.

Say, *"I AM fearlessly living and loving in a spirit of wellness."*

Imagine your lumbar vertebra and its structure: your lower back, from the back of your stomach and sides all the way down to your pelvis.

How do you feel about your hips, your tongue, your lower back, your genitals and your lower abdomen?

Briefly write it down.

Today, casually think about your posture and how you carry these parts of your physique.

Exercise	Sets	Reps	Percentage	Rest	Comments
Warm-up and Stretching					
Superset: Decline Bench Press Lunges	3	12-15	55-60%1RM	15 seconds	
Superset: Lat-Pulldown DB Stiff-leg DL	3	12-15	"	15 Seconds	
Superset: Seated DB Press Front Squat	3	12-15	"	15 seconds	
Superset: BB Curls Dips	3	12-15	"	15 seconds	
Abdominals: Inchworm	1	10			

Tuesday
DAY THREE

Starting Position: Stand in front of the mirror in the buff, and look into your eyes. Then look at the rest of you.

Action: Relax. Take a deep breath; imagine it going down to your navel. Look at your entire physique. Think about your chest, shoulders, upper back and arms, and your skin. Imagine through your heart and lungs you can give breath to all your desires. How does this feel? What are your desires?

Say, *"I AM inviting the Cosmic wisdom to fully*

touch and flow through my physique as light."

Are your shoulders squared or rounded? Why? Sit, breathe deeply and listen to your breath and your heartbeat. How do you feel about guilt? What do you think about guilt? Do you believe guilt can influence your posture? Is it affecting yours?

Briefly write it down.

Exercise	**Sets**	**Reps**	**Percentage**	**Rest**	**Comments**
Warm-up and Stretching					
Superset: Low-Incline DB Press Bent-over DB Row	4	10-12	55-60%1RM	15 seconds	
Superset: Chest-Supported Row (Machine) Leg Curl	4	10-12	"	15 seconds	
Superset: Standing Lateral raise Leg Extension	4	10-12	"	15 seconds	
Superset: Alternate DB Curl Triceps Pulldown	4	10-12	"	15 seconds	
Abdominals: Sit-up	1	10			

Wednesday
DAY FOUR

Starting Position: Stand in front of the mirror in the buff, and look at your nose, ears, neck, and throat area.

Action: Breathe. Imagine the breath through your nose and ears, down your throat, through your chest and abdomen area to your navel. Then up and out through your mouth. Repeat several times.

Say, *"Spirit Force, let this new **energy** spread through my heart—giving me peace at every start."*

Think about the impact your words have on you and others. How do you feel about the words humility, being wrong, gentleness, and patience in regards to others and yourself?

Briefly write it down.

Exercise	Sets	Reps	Percentage	Rest	Comments
Warm-up and Stretching					
Superset: Bench Press DB Bent-over Row	3	8-10	55-60%1RM	15 seconds	
Superset: Bench Push-up DB Rear Deltoid Fly	3	8-10	Body weight Light weight	15 seconds	
Superset: Military Press	3	8-10	55-60%	15 seconds	

Upright Row					
Superset: Cable curls Cable Triceps Extension	3	8-10	"	15 seconds	
Abdominals: Inchworm	1	10			

Thursday

DAY FIVE

Starting Position: Stand in front of the mirror in the buff.

Action: Breathe. Relax. Imagine your temple area while looking into your eyes. Next, gently close your eyes and see yourself with your spiritual eyes.

Say, *"Vivacious living, vibrate me—maintaining my strength to constructively do, speak, think, and to just be my best."*

How do you feel about your eyes and the area immediately surrounding your eyes: your brain, your mind, your forehead, and your thoughts? Do you look directly into other's eyes?

Then sit, taking in a few deep breaths, and exhaling with long slow sighs. Now begin to write, how you feel and think about the way you've been living? Are you equally taking care of yourself and the well-being of others?

REST Abdominals **CHEERS!!** **Increase Your Carbohydrate Intake (CARB-UP) for the remainder of the week.**	**COMMENTS**

Friday

DAY SIX

Starting Position: Stand in front of the mirror in the buff, and look closely at yourself.

Action: Take deep breaths. Imagine the breaths going all the way down and through your navel. Exhale all the air from your physique. Think about your posture. Relax. Imagine a triangle that extends from your upper abdominals down both sides of your waist and pointing to your navel. Breathe.

Say, *"Your full name, I salute you, and I thank you through and through!"*

How do you feel about the process of eating: the chewing, the swallowing, the digestion, the metabolism, and the elimination?

Briefly write it down.

Think about this: Fear and food can be used violently like rape. Rape is not really about sex. It's about domination and power. Both overwhelm the body's ***energy*** systems—physically, mentally, spiritually, and emotionally traumatic—resulting in shame and guilt, which are also damaging. Therefore, our sex, our fear, our food, and our conditional love become substitutes for power. ***Energy*** used to block our feelings to fill ourselves up and to express anger, confusion, limitation, and violence against ourselves.

Saturday OFF
DAY SEVEN

- You have watched your physique transform into a healthier channel for greater expression of your mind, heart, and soul. Remain dedicated and disciplined to the best of your ability.

Affirmation: I AM living the Rhythmic Training Dance precepts to cease wasting time and mental ***energy*** trying to find someone else to be accountable for my beauty, my health, and my harmony. I choose to cleanly squat, push, lift, and press on to preserve my strength, fear-free thinking, mobility, flexibility, and endurance, as well as my fat percentage with loving discipline and dedication.

Starting Position: Stand in front of the mirror in the buff.

Action: Twirl. Relax. Sit. Focus on your improvement in fearlessness, strength, alignment, endurance, body awareness, and appreciation. Are you balanced? What has changed?

Say how you feel and what you think about **your lovely self.**

Completely bask in and enjoy your contracted reward!

EPILOGUE

Continue changing, dancing, and evolving! Give thanks for the milestones, successes, and insights you have experienced so far, and send positive thoughts and prayers to your fellow travelers along the expedition to relaxing, releasing, and letting go on gravitational spaceship Earth. Remember:

- With inactivity—mental, physical or spiritual—there is no discomfort and therefore no progress and no growth. Remember the final principle of training, the Principle of Reversibility: "If you don't use it, you lose it."
- Loss of spiritual and physiological performance adaptations occur rapidly when a person terminates participation in regular training and meditation.

I pray that everyone can know this kind of love and be healed through it. If this prayer is read and heard, I will have fulfilled my duty to pass on what I've learnt in releasing all anchors to live painless and free. For the love of my son and my ex-fiancé, I am blessed and can only be grateful. Like the Kayapó, you can laugh and learn to live fearlessly with the promise of life—in love with your deep scars.

I know the voyage of diving in and swimming in the depth of your mind, body, and spirit can seem arduous. But I know that this voyage is the most important one you can ever make while prosperously experiencing life with the perseverance, the courage, and the freedom of managing the ***energy*** of your own mind!

BIBLIOGRAPHY

Ball, John. (1990). *Understanding Disease.* Essex, United Kingdom. C.W. Daniel.

Borba, Jonathan: Chapter Eight photographer credit.

Borysenko, Joan. (1998). *Minding the Body, Minding the Mind.* New York, NY. Bantum Dell.

Dennis, M., Visual imagery and the use of mental practice in the development of motor skills. Can. J. Applied Sport Science.10, 4s-16s.

Dossey, Dr. Larry. (1993). *Healing Breakthrough: How Attitudes and Beliefs Can Affect Your Health.* Essex, United Kingdom. Judy Piatkus Publishers Ltd.

Freedman, M.R., King J, K.E. (2001). *Popular diets: A scientific review.* Obesity Research.9:1S-40S.

Heyward, V.H. (2010). *Advanced Fitness Assessment and Exercise Prescription (6th ed.).* Champaign, IL. Human Kinetics.

Jequir, E. (2002). *Leptin signaling, adiposity, and energy balance.* Annual of the New York Academy of Sciences.379-88.

Kabal-Zinn, Jon. (1990). *Full Catastrophe Living.* New York, NY. Delacorte Press

Magil, R.A. (2007). *Motor Learning and Control (8thed.).* New York, NY. McGraw Hill

Martini, F.H. (2006). *Fundamentals of Anatomy & Physiology (7thed.).* San Francisco, CA: Pearson Education, Inc/Benjamin Cummings.

McArdle, W.D., Katch, F.I. & Katch, V.L.(2010). *Exercise Physiology, Nutrition, Energy and Human Performance (7thEd.).* Baltimore, MD. Wolteus Kluwer/Lippincott Williams & Williams

MedicineNet.com

Naess, Inger. (1996). *Colour Energy*. Canada. Rainbow Press

Wuest, D.A., Fisette, J.L. (2012). *Foundations of Physical Education, Exercise Science, and Sport (17th Ed.)*. New York, NY. McGraw Hill

ACKNOWLEDGMENTS

"Acknowledgment" is too astringently grating to appropriately thank the grace, the patience, the kindness and the consideration that has been given, asking nothing, enthusiastic to help the work prosper, and the intensity of my gratitude can certainly not be captured by a few brief words. Nonetheless, I can at least document that I most humbly thank you one and all.

ABOUT ATMOSPHERE PRESS

Atmosphere Press is an independent, full-service publisher for excellent books in all genres and for all audiences. Learn more about what we do at atmospherepress.com.

We encourage you to check out some of Atmosphere's latest releases, which are available at Amazon.com and via order from your local bookstore:

Eat to Lead, nonfiction by Luci Gabel
An Ambiguous Grief, a memoir by Dominique Hunter
My Take On All Fifty States: An Unexpected Quest to See 'Em All, nonfiction by Jim Ford
Geometry of Fire, nonfiction by Paul Warmbier
In the Cloakroom of Proper Musings, a lyric narrative by Kristina Moriconi
Chasing the Dragon's Tail, nonfiction by Craig Fullerton
Pandemic Aftermath: How Coronavirus Changed Global Society, nonfiction by Trond Undheim
My Cemetery Friends: A Garden of Encounters at Mount Saint Mary in Queens, New York, nonfiction and poetry by Vincent J. Tomeo
Change in 4D, nonfiction by Wendy Wickham
Disruption Games: How to Thrive on Serial Failure, nonfiction by Trond Undheim
Eyeless Mind, nonfiction by Stephanie Duesing

ABOUT THE AUTHOR

By formal education, N.Y. Haynes, MSc, holds dual degrees in Adaptive Eduation and Physiology. By passion, what she does supremely well is guiding and inspiring others to live healthier. Her practice as a health consultant and spiritual advisor offering her services to individuals around the world continues to be an exploration of the connectedness of all things. Learn more contact: 1greatfulgoddess@gmail.com

CPSIA information can be obtained
at www.ICGtesting.com
Printed in the USA
LVHW040850241120
672561LV00001B/154